How to Coach Basketball's 2-2-1 Penetration Offense

JAY SCHOFIELD

Parker Publishing Company, Inc.

West Nyack, New York

Library of Congress Cataloging in Publication Data

Schofield, Jay.
  How to coach basketball's 2-2-1 penetration
offense.

  Includes index.
  1. Basketball—Offense. 2. Basketball coaching.
I. Title. II. Title: How to coach basketball's
two-two-one penetration offense.
GV889.S36   796.32'32   81-22287
                AACR2

ISBN 0-13-403741-3

DEDICATION

TO: My wonderful wife, Pat, who doubles as our family's co-coach and my best friend.

TO: Our children, Shawn, Scott, and Sharlene, who work hard to make their co-coaches proud of them.

TO: My great parents, James and Geneva, for their love and support of their sons in all of our efforts.

TO: Marilyn, for her friendship and love of our family.

ACKNOWLEDGMENTS

To Leo Miller, Head Basketball Coach at Nauset Regional High School, who gave me my start in coaching and continues to be an excellent coach and fine friend.

To my former assistant coaches, Mike O'Brien and Roger Lemenager, who gave sound advice during this book's development.

To Michael McCarthy, former player and current Athletic Director, who best symbolizes all the fine gentlemen I've coached over the years at Martha's Vineyard and elsewhere.

To the many coaches I've heard speak at clinics and those whose articles I've read that have helped contribute to my knowledge of the game.

To the Good Lord, who is my Coach-of-the-Year every year.

How the 2-2-1 Penetration Offense Can Help Your Team

The futuristic 2-2-1 Penetration Offense has given modern offensive basketball a new face. To "penetrate" is to "pierce through," and this high-powered attack does just that to today's multiple defenses. Its two distinctive features are, first, an alignment unfamiliar to the defense, and second, a forceful inside triple posting game that creates a daring "try and stop us" team personality.

Any scoring attack, regardless of player alignment, will be successful if the players can execute the basic offensive principle. The scoring concepts stressed in the Penetration Offense are: good shots close to the basket, simple movements with safe passing lanes, offensive board domination, and the steady occupation of weakside defenders regardless of defensive structure.

These features, combined with the unique 2-2-1 set, have provided much success for our Penetration Offense. When you first see the set, it's hard to believe anything so simple can be so effective. The 2-2-1's unusual positions force defenders either to give strict individual coverage, which allows easily entered post passes, or to allow excessive freedom for both guards. These two defensive liabilities reduce the help and recover zoning principles inherent in most recent defenses.

Two guards operating from the top of the key, through the wing area, and down to the baseline require firm defensive attachment. The two forwards, beginning at the high post area and extending no further than 15 feet from the basket, pose additional singular coverage. The remaining baseline player generally goes box to box with some moves to the side and high-post areas. There is minimal low-post help here as the other offensive players are positioned too close to the basket.

How can this exceptional offense help your team? Many coaches are annually blessed with great players. Most teams, however, have only rare cycles of such talent. The usual turnout reveals players with average skills and limited size. If you, as coach, have mediocre talent you must control the game offensively. This helps you defensively because you are not constantly giving up the ball. The nature of this exceptional 2-2-1 set and its lane-perimeter balance actually confuses defenses as it capitalizes on your available talent.

The 2-2-1's adaptability to all levels of play is an added feature. High school coaches can easily incorporate this team-oriented offense into junior high feeder schools, since only the guard or forward positions need to be learned. This frees limited practice time for more fundamentals. It's a sound offense to teach; many offensive maneuvers are used that will promote your team's defensive awareness.

The 2-2-1 is also easily explained in this book; each chapter's primary focus is followed by a logical progression of related, competitive breakdown drills, rather than a catch-all drill chapter at the end of the book.

The 2-2-1 offense has other distinguishing features of particular interest to the discerning coach seeking an ultramodern scoring approach.

THE PENETRATION OFFENSE
NULLIFIES HELP-SIDE DEFENDERS

It evens up the prevailing 5 on 3 defensive advantage that many teams strive for. Its unusual set, relentless screens, and quick cuts keep all defenders busy. Defensive cheating is further reduced as all players operate from within their scoring range and stay but one pass away from a good shot. The 2-2-1's equal ball distribution also locates weak or foul-prone defenders.

THE 2-2-1 IS A POWER-POST ATTACK
WITH SUPPLEMENTARY GUARD HELP

Today's motion offenses have as a primary rule the ball being posted once every five or six passes in order to collapse the defensive perimeter. The ball is then returned to the guards for either shots or weakside reversals.

Conversely, the Penetration Offense's goal is to post the ball and leave it posted with three active players performing a variety of quick screens and cuts. The ball is sent out of the inside rotation only as a last resort and reentered as soon as possible. This places unyielding offensive pressure on both lane and perimeter defenders.

THE 2-2-1 BLENDS
SIMPLICITY WITH FLEXIBILITY

It stresses the effective movements of pattern play, yet encourages the frequent one-on-one opportunities within its structure. Coaches enjoy its strong execution and many options, yet their players see a chance for individual expression within the designated Penetration positions. This is like allowing a small child out to play but restricting him to the front yard. The offense mutually satisfies coach and players.

THE NEW 2-2-1 SET
ATTACKS ALL MULTIPLE DEFENSES

Today's advanced defenses are based on alternately showing, then closing down the seemingly available passing lanes. The 2-2-1 triple post alignment restricts defenders from trapping or hedging moves and forces them to stay at home. Its greatest strength may be its ability to adjust to any defense.

Penetration teams welcome all presses; they can confidently destroy them by using the trap-splitting Lineup Press Offense. The "net result" is usually just that ... a fan-appealing 3 on 2 fast-break finish for two points.

THE 2-2-1's PENETRATION
FORCES GAME TEMPO

Game rhythm is based on the team's ability to control the ball— whether it is off the boards, on the floor, or in the passing lanes. The 2-2-1 combines a crashing board command with a safe, low turnover, passing game. It can be played as either a quick-penetrating, shot-producing offense or a slowdown approach using patient, precise shot selection.

THE 2-2-1's EMPHASIS ON POSTING DISTORTS OPPONENTS' DEFENSES

The 2-2-1 forces the opponents to have at least three equally skilled post defenders. We have even posted exceptional guards in our 2-2-1 to further probe our opponents' weaknesses.

Statistics prove that teams win consistently only if they earn more lane shots than their opponents. The 2-2-1, with its vertical action, gives purposeful movement for each player as it posts the ball, forces fouls through its chosen shot selection, and controls the game's tempo with board dominance and ball control.

The Penetration Offense's disciplined flexibility forces a constant attack on modern multiple defenses. It is comprehensive enough to serve any team's needs. Although sophisticated, the pattern is easily learned as are its special options. Cohesive team play and offensive discipline are its natural byproducts.

Coaches adopting this novel 2-2-1 Penetration Offense as either a total scoring system or simply as a change-up secondary attack will soon agree, without question, that this is the offense of the future.

Jay Schofield

Table of Contents

CHAPTER 1:

The Penetration Offense— Building the Foundation

Coaching a basketball team is like building a skyscraper. The builder could place the first few stories slightly out of line and very few people would ever notice. But when the building reaches 20 stories high, everyone will notice that it tilts and won't hold up well under any real stress.

Basketball teams also must be developed very carefully in order to reach their maximum efficiency. This deliberate approach begins with the selection of those people directly involved with the team. When stresses arrive, we must be surrounded with quality people in order to enjoy success and to withstand hard times. These qualtiy people must be on the team as well as on the coaching staff.

THE COACHING STAFF

There are many concerns when selecting assistant coaches. On the high school level, there is often little choice as to the qualities of an assistant coach. These areas of competence become much more meaningful when hiring on the more competitive college level.

The ideal assistant coach is one who is working toward eventually becoming a head coach. He must be willing to speak his opinion freely and not be a "yes" man.

It is also very helpful if your assistant coach comes from another area of the country. This brings a new set of experiences for the head coach. The newcomer has undoubtedly seen many different theories of offense, defense, or game strategies not seen locally.

SELECTING THE PLAYERS

When choosing team members for the Penetration Offense, it is vital that the *person* is chosen before the *player* is. This is the main key to a team's success and eventual happiness, regardless of the win-loss record. A winning combination involves a group of quality people with basketball talent, who are willing to sacrifice some of their individuality for the good of the team.

There are certain types of players that fit best into a team's

---

MARTHA'S VINEYARD BASKETBALL

"A Person First, A Player Second"

Player Information Sheet

Name _____ Date _____

Age _____ Date of Birth _____ Grade _____ Ht. _____

Address _____ Phone _____

Parents or Guardian _____

Present Courses	Teacher	First Term Grades
1.		
2.		
3.		
4.		
5.		
6.		
7.		

DIAGRAM 1-1A

system of pattern play, such as the 2-2-1 attack. Some team members play only for fan response. Others will play for their individual statistics. Still others play to satisfy their egos. Good players will play basically to please their teammates. The great player, however, is one who simply seeks perfection in his game. Some players may fit into several of these groups. Others may transfer into different categories based on coaching.

Many players absorb coaching like sponges, while others won't. Because of their egos, some players are simply not coachable. Basketball, being such a tremendous ego sport, demands that all players submerge their individual egos into that of the team. The coach must then extract each player's excellence while channeling their egos into a common direction.

Although some players express themselves better than others, it is helpful to the coach if they can provide some information about themselves by means of a questionnaire. Some of this information is

---

Vertical Jump _____

Hotshot Score _____

Free Throw Score _____

List four teammates you'd like most to play with:

1. _____

2. _____

3. _____

4. _____

What are your season goals?

_____

_____

_____

In your opinion, who are our easiest league opponents?

1. _____ 2. _____

In your opinion, who are our toughest league opponents?

1. _____ 2. _____

DIAGRAM 1-1B

objective in nature but the remainder may provide clues concerning a player's individual feelings and those toward his potential teammates. This chart is shown in Diagrams 1-1A and 1-1B. It is usually on a 5″ x 8″ index card and is filled out on both sides.

During team tryouts, regardless of the methods used, certain steps must be taken to ensure that each player gets a fair chance to make the team. Conversely, the coach must be able to spot troubles before they appear. Some superior players end up as problem athletes who are capable of affecting a team's performance. Such players must be released. Here a coach can add by subtracting. A coach must also closely examine any "dark horses" who have great attitudes. These players will push the top seven all year.

Many coaches prefer that their players concentrate on basketball during the off-season. We feel it is vital that our athletes play other sports in order to develop intensity throughout the entire season. Many ballplayers get tired of the game just when they should be peaking in late February.

Another reason for taking all-around athletes is that in addition to developing their competitive fires, they are also getting a strong feeling for the big rivalries with certain teams that exist in the local conferences or leagues.

Teach the 2-2-1's breakdown drills during tryouts. This helps to evaluate the "coachability" of each player. Full-court man defensive drills must also be used to judge the player's competitive nature during full scrimmage action. During this full-court competition, our managers keep the game charts that pinpoint each player's strengths or weaknesses. This charted information may then be used when having personal conferences with those players who are cut. Team lists that are posted create nothing but an empty, lonely feeling for the player whose name is missing. You should temporarily pretend that this "cut" youngster is your own child and treat him accordingly.

THE BENCH

Because the Penetration Offense uses only guards and forwards, the bench is easy to organize and rely upon. Two positions, rather than the normal three, make it simple to substitute.

A sound bench is the key to the preparation for each game. When they are playing a good, consistent game, they create alertness and aggressiveness for the first seven or eight players. They contribute directly to our season, in that, several times during a season, some have to come off the bench and perform like starters. Because of our 2-2-1 set requiring only two positions, we can also afford to vary our starting lineup often in order to develop more of a "family" feeling. It is critical to start many different players in today's game, because they all want a "piece of the action." Clearly, the bench must be more than just a place to sit if a team plans to win more than they lose.

THE 2-2-1 PENETRATION OFFENSE

Positioning the 2-2-1

Basketball's offensive sets have been constantly changing during the game's development. The original and most popular alignment involved two guards, two forwards, and a center in a standard 2-1-2 alignment. Coaches began experimenting and the 1-2-2 and 1-3-1 sets soon evolved. Eventually, the 1-4 and double stack arrived, but not without constant criticism from the game's "purists."

Popular acceptance of these sets soon became commonplace as coaches selected their scoring attacks based on available talent. The 2-2-1 set is the latest in offensive attacks and will soon gain popularity as did the others.

A coach must develop an offensive philosophy that includes the decision to use either one or two guards. I was once a firm advocate of a single guard offense for many seasons until the disadvantages outweighed advantages.

A supposed benefit of the single guard offense involved the wings being denied the ball. This alignment reduced the helpside defense and invited backdoor scoring chances. After drilling on backdoor plays and then examining our point returns, I discovered that backdoor opportunities didn't really produce many points. Our point guards weren't capable of throwing that perfect pass needed to hit the cutter. Those few passes that did get through often resulted in a charge earned by a well-drilled helpside defensive forward.

Also, one great defender can nullify the efforts of the single guard. This can destroy the total offense, since the defender will pressure the guard to the point of stopping the dribble, which makes the entry pass too long. Once stopped, the passer is then harassed to the point of not making a crisp, accurate pass. A single guard may, out of necessity, be forced to dribble excessively, which increases standing time for his teammates. With two guards, there is limited dribbling in setting up the offense.

Two guards are better than one to relieve strong defensive pressure applied to a single guard. With two guards, the guard with the inferior defender brings the ball upcourt and begins the offense. Two guards with average ability are easier for a coach to find (or develop) than one guard with outstanding ability. This, again, makes substitution easier as more guards can play due to less specialization.

The 2-2-1's structure is further simplified by requiring only guard and forward positions. This separation makes practice very efficient, as positional breakdown drills can be easily managed by two coaches each drilling a separate position.

Forwards' Operational Areas. The high forward's placement in the post area is difficult to defend. Most coaches teach defending from behind this high post. Others provide only passive defense as the high post player can't score until he pivots and faces the basket. Diagram 1-2 shows the four possible forward positions being occupied by the 2-2-1 forwards.

Additionally, the high elbow area is an especially tough area to defend, as the guard's dribbling movement can move the post defender. In an effort to discourage the post pass, the defensive post's moves have often resulted in fouls prior to the ball being passed. Defenders know that the Penetration Offense, once started, can score well, so their efforts are directed toward stopping all entry passes.

Our forwards are generally restricted to operating in these four designated areas of both low posts and the high post elbow spots at the ends of the foul line. We will develop special plays if these

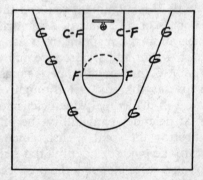

DIAGRAM 1-2
Operational Areas

forwards have other abilities allowing them scoring effectiveness outside the lane.

Guards' Operational Areas. The 2-2-1 guards' operational areas extend from the top of the key toward the baseline, as shown in Diagram 1-2. They are always within their shooting range from the basket unless they have an exceptional posting talent. Such talent may find them taking weak defenders to one of the forward's post spots for special scoring plays.

PLAYING WITH OR
WITHOUT THE CENTER

The chances of having a true center are usually slim. Potential forwards are more likely to surface and then be motivated if the player has any aspirations of competing on the college level. Most high school centers must make the transition to forward once they begin playing on the college level.

The Penetration Offense is versatile enough to accommodate the talents of an available center-type player. This player is often referred to in subsequent chapters as a *center-forward*. He usually starts in the low-post area just above the block. Special plays are designed for his power skills, although they seldom take him out of the lane area. The center-forward's (C-F) beginning positions are shown in Diagram 1-2.

ADJUSTING TO A
THREE-GUARD OFFENSE

If a team finds that it is going to be small and that there will be an abundance of guards, it must then adjust the 2-2-1 to score effectively. This can be done a number of ways.

The strongest guard can be converted to a forward, who can fill one of the high elbow posts. If the guard is a good inside scorer, he can drop down to the low post and then overpower his defender from in close.

On the other hand, a quick and penetrating guard can use his one-on-one skills from this high post spot. See Diagram 1-3.

Yet another option is to run the Cross Lane Continuity, which is run by using three guards with two forwards This offense is described entirely in Chapter 4. Diagram 1-3A shows the third guard in the low post.

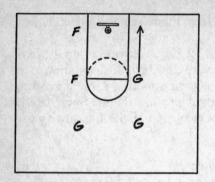

DIAGRAM 1-3
Strong or Quick Guard
Posted High

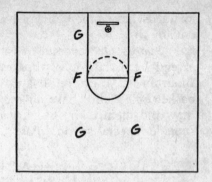

DIAGRAM 1-3A
Cross Lane Set
with Three Guards

QUALITIES OF THE 2-2-1 GUARD

Adequate guard skills are critical to the execution of any efficient offense. Such skills must be developed methodically so that each guard can handle all game situations confidently. Most areas are mentioned here, but they will be covered in greater detail in further chapters.

Dribbling

Guards must have good dribbling skills in order to penetrate into the scoring and passing areas. All change-of-direction dribbles are practiced constantly with a special emphasis on not putting the dribbler's back to his defenders. The *spin* or *whirl* dribble is discouraged, as today's run and jump defenses are made more effective when they defend a two-guard front. There is little risk in the defender trying to double-up on the ball as the guard's release pass is generally not a penetrating pass. We devote a lot of practice time while stressing either the crossover or behind-the-back dribble. Both of these moves still allow the guard to look upcourt and "see the rim." This is our teaching phrase for dribbling. If the dribber can see the rim, he can see his teammates.

Passing

The other half of ball-handling is passing. This facet of the modern game is often neglected. Coaches do a great job in teaching sound defensive strategies which, in turn, have overpowered today's unpracticed passing skills. Young players, when involved in "pickup" games, generally concentrate only on shooting and one-on-one solo efforts against a weak defense. As a result, the minimum passing that is done is accomplished with little resistance.

The guards are drilled on the various passing "planes" and how the nearest defender dictates which pass will be thrown. The two basic "planes" or "holes" are the defender's shoulders and knees. We teach faking toward one passing plane and then actually delivering the ball through the other open plane. In general, we pass away from the defender's hands. The holes, or planes, are shown in Diagram 1-4. The two holes opposite the hands are always open. When passing, the ball is faked quickly toward either of the defender's hands and then thrown through the open hole. This fake tends to "freeze" the defender's hands into position and briefly reinforce his thought that the ball is coming toward that hand.

This little teaching tool helps reduce careless passing, which is usually due to a lack of concentration. This passing plane theory is part of the general objective of teaching the ball handlers to make their passes "away from the defenders," not "toward their teammates." Many guards don't read the defensive position well and feel that the defensive player is out of intercepting range. This results in steals or deflected passes.

Passing opportunities last but a split second. If the passer doesn't see his open teammate at that instant, he must then make a less desirable pass.

Shooting

The guards are taught their own individual shooting ranges. Most players are unrealistic concerning their game-shooting limits and must be reminded often just what constitutes good shot selection. Intelligent shot selection is based primarily on three areas: distance, defensive pressure, and confidence of delivery.

The Penetration Offense focuses on getting the ball posted in the lane area and keeping it there by using numerous cuts and screens. Once the ball is posted, the guards must stay within their shooting limits. They should be able to shoot from outside if their defensive guards drop off to help out on the inside posting action. The shooting drills used by the guards are concentrated in the wing and baseline areas.

DIAGRAM 1-4

QUALITIES OF THE 2-2-1 FORWARD

The three forwards are the true heart of the 2-2-1 Penetration Offense. They must be skilled in many areas but those especially critical are receiving passes, driving one-on-one, inside shooting, and setting strong screens. Those areas are briefly touched upon here but will be covered in greater detail in Chapter Three.

Receiving Post Passes

The offense usually starts with the guard's post pass to either of the high forwards. Some defenders actively challenge this pass, while others allow it and then play tough defense following the post's square-up pivot move.

If the post defender doesn't challenge the post pass, the post man presents a two-handed target area for the passing guard. This broad target serves to keep the defender away from the passing lane. This position also reinforces the stance we insist on for rebounding. The hands are also wide so that the post can quickly adjust toward a bad pass, should one be thrown, from a strongly pressured guard.

If a post defender actively tries to deny the pass, we teach a *seal* move designed to free the post for all passes. This seal move is adjustable to any of the designated posting areas.

If a post player is to be effective as a pass receiver, he must be physically strong and quick enough to catch a variety of passes thrown his way. We deliberately throw him bad as well as good passes in practice and vary the speeds of these passes. This is done in an effort to develop his hands. We also experiment with throwing him different-sized athletic balls in practice sessions to improve his visual skills while "seeing the ball" into his hands. These drills, teaching theories, and the above-mentioned sealing techniques will be further developed in detail in Chapter Three.

Driving

The forward must recognize when a defender is playing him too closely. This makes the defender extremely susceptible to a drive on a cleared-out side of the lane. One dribble separates him from a lay-up and a possible three-point opportunity from the helpside defensive forward.

After receiving the ball and squaring up to the basket, the forward instantly assumes the standard triple threat position. He is then able to use the one-on-one moves that are also detailed in Chapter Three.

Inside Shooting

The players are drilled on several basic shots within the lane area. These are all designed to attack the defenders aggressively and to make the forwards extremely conscious of the three-point play. This offensive philosophy gets rid of interior defenders or at least reduces their effectiveness. Positional shots and drills are taught separately in Chapter Three.

A move especially valuable to the 2-2-1's inside players is the *pump fake*. The crucial part of this movement is that the head and the ball must be moved together. This motion will nullify today's eager shotblockers because it destroys their timing. Many young players equate great defense with "rejecting" ability. This often works to the shooter's advantage, since he can earn three-point plays while putting some key opponents in foul trouble. The pump fake is best taught by using the visual example of an imaginary wire connecting the ball and the shooter's jaw. Tell your players that, as the ball is faked upward, the head is also "pulled" upward through the same distance. The pump fake is less deceptive if only the ball is shown and the head doesn't move.

Screens

The forwards must be adept at setting strong screens. The team benefits greatly from solid "hits" down low in the lane. A sloppy screen is wasted motion that allows the defense easy routes while staying with their assigned men. Screeners must be constantly reminded and drilled in the setting of legal screens. Hands and arms must be in close to the body. When using a front screen, the hands should be used over the crotch area to protect the groin. It is best to firmly grasp one wrist with the other hand to lock both elbows, which will give a legal screen. The screener's body must also not bend unnaturally sideways at the hip when trying to "hang up" a defender.

IMPLEMENTING THE PENETRATION SELF-IMPROVEMENT PROGRAM

Players are developed during the off-season months, whereas the team, itself, is built from November through March. We tell our players that if they work hard to become the best possible players they can be then the staff will do their job of getting them in shape and blending their talents into the best team possible.

Karate has a system of awarding different-colored belts for reaching graduated levels of achievement. Why couldn't a similar idea be devised for basketball? This program could motivate the players to work in the off-season toward greater skill development.

One of the most obvious methods to show a player's outstanding achievements is the use of different-colored sneaker laces. This uniform award system is comparable to football players earning various decals to wear on their game helmets.

Our regular school colors are purple and white. All players must wear white laces until they can earn their "color" and get placed on

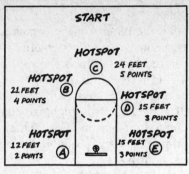

SCORING	HOTSHOT RULES	POINTS
Lay-up	(Only Two Scores Allowed)	2
Hotspot A	(12 Feet from Basket Left Corner)	2
Hotspot B	(21 Feet from Basket Left of Key)	4
Hotspot C	(24 Feet from Basket Top of Key)	5
Hotspot D	(15 Feet from Basket Right of Key)	3
Hotspot E	(15 Feet from Basket Right Corner)	3
Bonus	(Attempting Shots from All Five Hotspots)	3

DIAGRAM 1-5

1. A shot made from any Hotspot is worth the number of points allotted to that particular spot. (See the points marked next to each spot on the diagram.)
2. Each player has one minute to score as many points as possible. (Someone keeps time, while someone else shoots.)
3. Starting at half court, the contestant dribbles as fast as possible into shooting range and shoots lay-ups or fires away from the Hotspots in any sequence he or she prefers. The contestant shoots as many shots as possible in one minute.
4. There are only two lay-up scores allowed (worth two points each). All other shots must be taken from any of the five Hotspots.
5. Three bonus points are awarded if a player shoots from all five Hotspots (regardless of whether he or she makes the basket).
6. When shooting from a Hotspot, a player must begin the actual shot with at least one foot touching any part of the spot.
7. One point is subtracted for each dribbling or motion violation (palming, traveling, double dribbling).
8. If the ball gets stuck between the basket and the backboard, time is stopped until the ball is retrieved. Play and time begins again at the same spot from where the player took the last shot.

one of two desirable levels. When a player reaches the first level, he is allowed to wear purple laces. The top step entitles the player to wear gold laces. These colored laces, which are supplied by the coaching staff, can be worn for practices and games.

The purple or gold lace steps are based on three levels of objective basketball achievement, which are challenging yet attainable through a dedicated off-season effort. These three areas are: (1) vertical (Sargent) jump; (2) Pepsi-Cola/NBA Hotshot scoring levels; and (3) a free throw shooting test.

The vertical jump is measured by having the player stand flat-footed and reach upward to make a chalk mark as high as he can against a wall. He then takes three consecutive jumps (no running starts are allowed) and makes a chalk mark on the wall as high as possible when at the peak of each leap. A yardstick is then used to measure the distance in inches between the standing and the three jumping marks. The highest measurement is then recorded as the player's vertical jumping height.

The Pepsi-Cola/NBA Hotshot is the second area of player competence that we measure in order to award colored laces. It is valid, quickly administered, and performance-tested for player popularity. Diagram 1-5 includes both the court and the rules for this second procedure used in awarding laces.[1]

The third and final portion of the color-lace program is achieved by having each player shoot 100 free throws. He shoots them in four sets of 25 per set while alternating with a teammate.

After the three tests are administered to each of the players, their scores are then compared with the designated scores on the Color Chart, as shown in Diagram 1-6. This chart also indicates at the bottom the required levels of achievement needed for all players who are trying to win either the purple or gold laces. These tables at the bottom can be adjusted either up or down based on your team's overall talent at each grade level. Exercise your judgment when setting demanding, yet realistic, scores.

A player must achieve all three scores at the appropriate class level in order to pass the test. For instance, a sophomore must have a vertical jump of 24," score at least 25 points in the Pepsi-Cola/NBA Hotshot, and make 65 of 100 free throws in order to get the gold laces for the season.

---

[1]Material reproduced with the permission of the copyright owner. ©PepsiCo, Inc., 1980. PEPSI, PEPSI-COLA, and HOTSHOT are registered trademarks of PepsiCo, Inc.

NAME	J U M P	Pepsi-Cola/ NBA Hotshot Score	Free Throws	NAME	J U M P	Pepsi-Cola/ NBA Hotshot Score	Free Throws
1.				9.			
2.				10.			
3.				11.			
4.				12.			
5.				13.			
6.				14.			
7.				15.			
8.				16.			

CLASS	Color	Jump	Pepsi-Cola/NBA Hotshot Score	Free Throws
Freshmen	Purple Gold	18″ 22″	15 pts. 20 pts.	50/100 55/100
Sophomores	Purple Gold	20″ 24″	20 pts. 25 pts.	60/100 65/100
Juniors	Purple Gold	22″ 26″	25 pts. 30 pts.	70/100 75/100
Seniors	Purple Gold	24″ 30″	30 pts. 40 pts.	80/100 90/100

DIAGRAM 1-6

The strength of this program is that it provides great incentive during the off-season. The players enjoy the challenge each year while working toward the colored laces. It is a visible symbol of achievement but not one so obvious that it takes away from the teamwork so necessary for winning basketball. We are very strict administering the testing procedures because we don't want to grant anything to a player that is undeserved. Such laxness would reduce the value of the awards received.

If a player passes one or two parts, but not the third, he can keep the two passing grades for the rest of the month while still attempting to pass the remaining portion. If he doesn't pass by the end of the month, he then loses his two passing grades and then must retest at the beginning of the month. This speeds up the testing process while keeping pressure on the player to maintain his skills. The lace system serves a great role in helping the players cope with stress while performing "in the clutch." It is true that we expect high performances from the players but they respond very well.

Our self-improvemement program is one that is designed with both guards and forwards in mind. It develops overall skills that directly benefit the players in their "lace chase" that means so much to them. The following is a copy of this program.

SELF-IMPROVEMENT PROGRAM

1. **DRIBBLING—BALL HANDLING**

   A. Dribbling
      1. Head and eyes up — see the rim — don't travel — be quick.
      2. Do one trip up the court and back again using each type of dribble as often as possible:
         (a) righty; (b) lefty; (c) crossover; (d) behind the back; (e) spin; (f) change of pace; (g) "show-time" (combination of all)
   B. Ball Handling
      1. Body circles (eight times)
      2. Figure-eight leg circles (eight times)
      3. Crab walk (full-court — up and back — one round trip)

2. **REBOUNDING**

   A. Toss the ball off the backboard and rebound it using four different types of rebounds:
      1. right-handed
      2. left-handed
      3. alternate right and left hands
      4. both hands
   B. Spend 3 minutes on each type of rebound for a total of 12 minutes.
   C. *TIPS:* Rebound by doing the following: Spread your legs out and bend from the waist. Extend the hands fully while catching the ball as high as you can.

3. **DEFENSIVE CLOCK SLIDES**

   A. Arrange clock positions with rocks (or chalk) on a 15′ circle. Set rocks at 12, 3, 6, and 9 o'clock positions.
   B. Start at 12 and shuffle back to 6, up to 1, back to 7, up to 2, back to 8, up to 3, over to 9, down to 4, up to 10, down to 5, up to 11, down to 6, and finish up at 12.

C. After your slide forward, (spots 1, 2, 3, 10, 11, and 12) have your hands up while pretending to guard an imaginary shooter.

D. *TIPS:* Maintain defensive stance and be quick from 12 to 12. Time yourself and try to decrease your time each day. Maintain a balanced defensive stance.

4. JUMPING-TIPPING

A. Jumping

1. Touch the rim, board, net, or some high object as many times in a row as possible before tiring. Try to get to 50 jumps in a row.

2. *TIPS:* Set a new goal number for yourself each time you work out. After you reach 50 straight, pick out a higher spot to jump for during your next series of workouts. Continue these steps and you'll find yourself both stronger and quicker regardless of your size.

B. Tipping

a. Tip the ball off the board six times in a row. Tip it in on the seventh time. Concentrate on quick jumping with little "gathering" of the hands and arms.

b. Make a total of 5 baskets the first time out. Next, add a basket each day until you are making 20 baskets each day.

5. LAY-UPS AND DRIBBLE MOVES

A. *TIPS*: Be quick; not casual—pump fake on every other shot — start from the top of the key and go game speed but stay under control of the ball and yourself — see the rim.

	Number of Times	Dribble Moves	Lay-ups
B.			
1.	10	Right	Right
2.	10	Left	Left
3.	5	Right, crossover	Left
4.	5	Left, crossover	Right
5.	5	Right, spin	Left
6.	5	Left, spin	Right
7.	5	Right, behind the back	Left
8.	5	Left, behind the back	Right
9.	5	Right, change of pace	Right
10.	5	Left, change of pace	Left

6. FREE THROWS

A. Shoot 100 free throws and record number of shots you made.

B. Follow all your misses. Tip or shoot the short jumper on misses.

C. Pump fake on all misses in the lane if you can't tip it in.

D. *TIPS:* Pretend all of your free throws are in overtime — never up; never in!

7. SHOOTING

A. Mix all six types of dribbles from the top of the key. Pretend some great pro defender is guarding you while you are dribbling and shooting.

B. Dribble to the following areas and *MAKE 25* jumpers from each spot: right baseline, left baseline, right wing, left wing, and along the free throw line.

    1. Follow all shots and either tip or grab and shoot all misses.

    2. Don't shoot at next area until 25 jumpers are made.

    3. Total number of shots made are 125 from your range. (This does not count your misses and tips).

8. PASSING

A. Use a wall or flat object to pass against.

B. Pass 100 times using chest pass and bounce pass alternately.

C. Pass through all four passing planes. Fake through one first and then pass through another.

D. *TIPS:* Gradually try to move further away from the wall and pass with good power, quickness, and realistic faking. Pass to a small target to improve your concentration.

It is good coaching to run these drills intermittently during the regular season so players will have confidence in them to run on their own.

This chapter sets the stage for the 2-2-1 Penetration Offense. At this point you should have a feeling for the 2-2-1's players and their basic positioning. The athletes' off-season development ideas are used here in conjunction with the 2-2-1 but could also be used with other offensive attacks.

The following chapters will be more easily understood now that the 2-2-1's beginnings and framework have been discussed.

CHAPTER 2:

Attacking Man Defenses with the 2-2-1 Triple Post

Today's man defenses, best exemplified by Coach Bobby Knight's Indiana University teams, are stronger than ever with their intense pressure on the ball, guard-forward denial, and helpside positioning.

A scoring philosophy with sound offensive concepts is needed to attack these defenses successfully. The 2-2-1's Five Penetration Principles, when specifically facing man defenses, are briefly discussed below.

FIVE PENETRATION PRINCIPLES

1. Player Movement

The 2-2-1 high-low triple post empties the baseline of all helpside defenders. All players have built-in incentives for good off-ball movement as the offense rewards them with the ball. Three receivers are always in shooting range for scoring passes if their off-ball cuts are well-executed. The 2-2-1's offensive theory stresses one player with the ball trying to give it up and four players without the ball trying to earn it.

2. Ball Movement

The 2-2-1's unique alignment creates safe, short passing lanes with few turnovers. Its continuous, inside ball movement with quickness of floor reversal lets the ball attack pressure quickly.

3. Offensive Rebounding

This set keeps three lane rebounders and a crashing guard available for many second shots. We know when the shot will be taken so anticipation plays a big key in beating box-outs. Defensive box-outs are especially difficult as the penetrating cuts give great knifing angles for our four crashing rebounders. Vertical team movement increases second shots.

4. Good Lane Shots

The 2-2-1's inside triangle is a sound cornerstone upon which to build an offense giving high percentage shots. The stress on early ball posting with frequent one-on-one situations from the patterns result in many close shots.

5. Equal Ball Distribution

The offense creates balanced team scoring, since all positions earn great shooting chances. The inside posting attack satisfies the forwards, yet the guards are well-placed to score often if their defenders sag for post help. Coaches using the Penetration Offense can be assured the ball will find the best shooter through constant team movement. All five players understand that they'll be presented with good shots.

PASS AND PICK ATTACK

The Pass and Pick Attack from the 2-2-1's triple post set is our basic scoring weapon against all man defenses.

Diagram 2-1 shows the starting alignment with players in their designated positions, as discussed in Chapter 1. To review, 1 and 2 are the guards, 3 and 4 are the high forwards, and 5 is either a third forward or center if one is available.

The Pass and Pick Attack is ignited as soon as the ball is posted at either high forward. Diagram 2-2 shows 2 making his entry pass to high forward 4 and following it with his wide vision cut to become the baseline guard. If the ball is posted at 3, 5 then crosses the lane, as shown in Diagram 2-3, and the offense is run identically. Player 5 must always stay opposite the first penetrating pass. Top guard 1 rotates to the center for defense. We call him our "goalie."

Player 2's vision cut, following his entry post pass, accomplishes several things.

PURPOSES OF VISION CUT

1. It occupies his defender all the way to the baseline, which eliminates defensive harassment on the high forward with the ball.
2. The finished cut places the guard within his baseline shooting range and facing the basket.
3. The vision cut was so named to graphically teach both the guard and forward mutual court vision and team awareness.

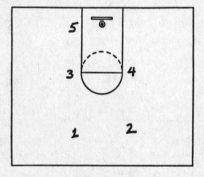

DIAGRAM 2-1
Basic Set

Post 4, with the ball, squares up to the basket using a front-facing pivot. If his defender is playing him too closely, he drives one-on-one on the cleared-out side. Diagram 2-4 shows this drive with 2's completed vision cut eliminating defensive help from his man. The only remaining possible help comes from the low defender on 5. This opens up the short drop-pass to 5 who quickly steps up into the lane facing the basket. This low seal in Diagram 2-5 places 3's dropping defensive post on 5's back. If the one-on-one doesn't develop, a 3 on 2 may be briefly available.

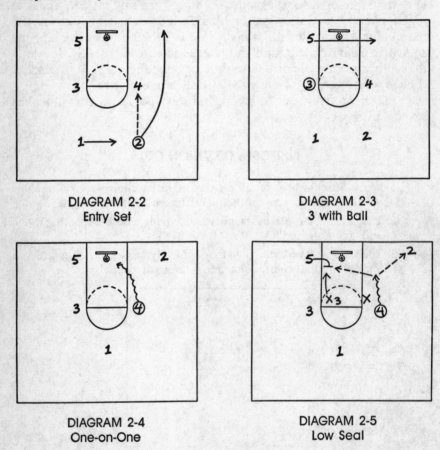

DIAGRAM 2-2
Entry Set

DIAGRAM 2-3
3 with Ball

DIAGRAM 2-4
One-on-One

DIAGRAM 2-5
Low Seal

PASS AND PICK ATTACK VS. MAN DEFENSE

Diagrams 2-6 and 2-7 show the Pass and Pick Attack with its continuity. When 3 sees that 4 didn't drive, he immediately starts the post attack by setting a headhunting downscreen on the low defensive player. Player 5 fakes a crosscut, then pops out hard off 3's downscreen looking for 4's pass, then a quick shot. Diagram 2-7 shows that 3, immediately on contact with the low defensive player, executes an "open-up" move to face the ball as he slides across the lane to the ball side. This quick open-up places the low defender on 3's back and keeps him there, providing that 3 opens up big with visible, high, and wide hand targets at head height. Both hands held high also show the officials there is no holding going on down low. It is also vital that, following the screen, 3 takes wide slide-steps across the lane for both speed and easy pass-receiving purposes. Player 4 looks to hit 3 directly at midlane but also has 2 and 5 as potential receivers.

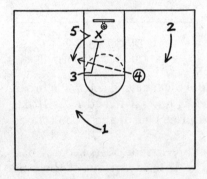

DIAGRAM 2-6
Downscreen

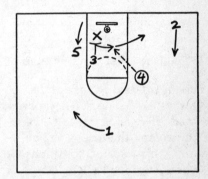

DIAGRAM 2-7
Open-up Move

If neither option is there, 5 comes higher to catch 4's pass. This is the critical timing area of the continuity as the phrase "Pass and Pick" is repeated over and over in practice until each of the three posts automatically passes first, then immediately picks down for the player on his side. Any reluctance on the screener's part may hang up the high forward with the ball and limit his options.

Often the receiver will be releasing his shot while his passer has already started toward the basket to set the downscreen. The low man on the screener's side yells "Shot!" as the screener continues down the lane, letting his momentum carry him to the midlane position of the rebounding triangle. Diagram 2-8 shows this movement as the three rebounders each fill a corner of the rebounding triangle. Player 2 also looks to rebound the weakside, as many missed shots result in rebounds opposite the shooter.

If no shot is taken by 5, the Pass and Pick Attack continues as shown in Diagram 2-9. Player 5 looks for 3 coming high off 4's downscreen. Player 4, following his screening contact on 3's man,

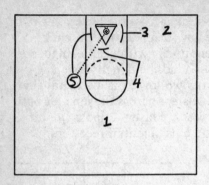

DIAGRAM 2-8
"Shot!" with Rebound Triangle

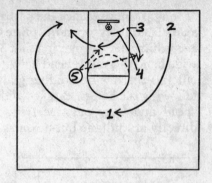

DIAGRAM 2-9
Pass and Pick Continuity

opens up; taking wide slide-steps across the lane and keeping a broad target for 5's pass. The guards, 1 and 2, have switched roles; 1 has made his vision cut to become the baseline guard, and 2 has rotated to become the defensive goalie.

This rotation continues with the three inside posts keeping ball possession for as long as possible. The ball is sent out of the post rotation to a guard only when absolutely necessary. It is then returned inside (if the guard doesn't have a good shot) and the posting continues with this series of picks, rolls, and pop outs.

It must be constantly stressed that the high post with the ball must continually read his defender's positioning. The 15-foot jumper is there if the post defender sags back to block the passing lanes. Conversely, if the defender swarms all over this high forward with the ball to block his passing vision, he is open to a one-on-one drive through the cleared-out side.

Teaching is simplified when each player knows his rules—especially in the early season. Even though it is a surprisingly easy offense to teach and learn, these guidelines simplify the coaching process. The following is a progressive order of action for all five positions.

Rules for the Baseline Guard

1. If your forward receives the ball, become the baseline guard by making the vision cut to the baseline (regardless of how your high forward got the post pass).

2. Finish your cut on the baseline within your shooting range but not so close as to crowd the lane area with an extra defender.

3. On a post's release pass to you, look to shoot immediately if open. If no shot is available, reenter the ball into a post as soon as possible.

Rules for the High Forward with the Ball

1. Drive the cleared-out side. You are but one dribble from a lay-up.
2. Shoot the 15-foot shot.
3. Hit the baseline guard with a pass.
4. Pass to the low forward coming off the downscreener across the lane.
5. Pass to the screener at midlane after his open-up move.
6. Release to the top guard and start over.

Rules for the Screening Forward

1. After passing to the pop-out forward, downscreen the same side you're on against the low defender.
2. On a shot by the high forward, the low forward will yell "Shot!", indicating that you must fill the midlane corner of the rebounding triangle.
3. Open up facing the ball with arms wide and hands at head height.
4. Expect the ball at midlane or on the other side of the lane.

Rules for the Low Forward

1. Fake the crosscut to set up your move; then cut hard off the downscreen, forcing a defensive switch. Pop out behind the screen expecting a pass.
2. On a shot attempt from the high forward, yell "Shot!" and fill the nearest rebounding triangle corner.
3. Expect the pass at the side post area and shoot if open.
4. If denied the cross-lane pass, come higher up the lane line to the elbow and receive the pass, keeping the rotation alive.
5. Run the backdoor to the other low post, if your defender is cheating high, to beat the approaching downscreen.

Rules for the Top Guard

1. If your forward doesn't receive the entry pass, rotate to the center area above the key for defensive balance as the goalie.
2. Serve as a release for the post, but reenter the ball inside as soon as possible.
3. On an inside ball reversal, (with the ball at your forward's high post cut) you become the baseline guard, making a wide vision cut.

THE DRIBBLE CROSS CONTINUITY

The Pass and Pick Attack capitalizes on strong forward play, but there are some nights when the guards meet severe man pressure while crossing the midcourt line. For this reason, we developed the Dribble Cross Continuity from the 2-2-1 penetration set. It is most effective for handling guards who dribble well with either hand and play sound two-man basketball.

Diagram 2-10 shows the 2-2-1 alignment. Guards 1 and 2 use a dribble exchange while advancing the ball against midcourt pressure. When facing any man pressure, guard 1 continues dribbling at an angle toward the opposite corner. Guard 2 crosses just in front of 1, hoping to loosen up some defensive pressure while emptying his half of the court for 1's drive.

This Dribble Cross, or exchange, is a signal for the forwards that this continuity will be run during this particular possession. Forward 4 sets a backscreen for guard 1 by executing a front-facing pivot. The screener faces his corner of the court to ensure a legal screen. Diagram 2-11 shows 1 and 4 playing the pick and roll as 3 makes a baseline fake to set up his defender for the flash pivot into 4's vacated forward spot. This is the first cut of the Dribble Cross Continuity. Guard 2 has rotated to become the top guard for defense and ball reversal. Baseline guard 1 now has several choices after the unsuccessful pick and roll possibility with 4. Player 3 is often open at 4's spot for a pass and short jumper. Player 4 posts low, then headhunts 5's defender in the lane. Player 5, after setting up his man, cuts either high or low off 4's screen as shown in Diagram 2-12. After the screen, 4 may pop quickly toward the ball but must then go opposite 5's cut and then must fill the weakside low post. This is the second move of the Dribble Cross.

Next, 2 receives the ball either by a direct swing pass from 1 or by a relay from 1 to 3 and then to 2. Diagram 2-12A shows both methods of ball reversal. Player 4 comes up the lane high to set yet another backscreen for the top guard 2 who plays the pick and roll game with him.

The Dribble Cross is run over again from the other side as shown in Diagram 2-13. Player 3 fakes down, then flashes up looking for the baseline guard's pass. Player 4, if not open on the pick and roll,

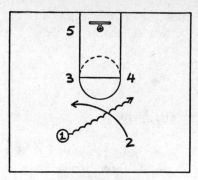

DIAGRAM 2-10
Dribble Exchange

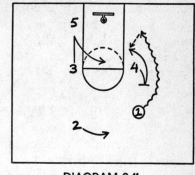

DIAGRAM 2-11
Pick and Roll

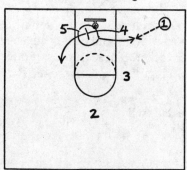

DIAGRAM 2-12
Headhunt Screen

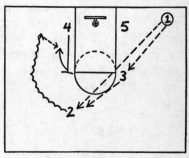

DIAGRAM 2-12A
Ball Reversal and Continuity
in Action

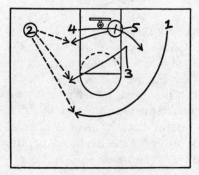

DIAGRAM 2-13
Completed Continuity

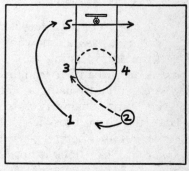

DIAGRAM 2-14
Cross Feed

headhunts 5's man in the lane as 5 comes either high or low looking for 2's pass. This simple, yet active guard series forces defensive movement while creating great offensive specialization for good screeners and drivers. It is an effective change-of-pace offense when varied with the Pass and Pick Attack.

FORWARD PRESSURE BREAKERS

The Dribble Cross series relieves tough pressure for guards but there is often additional pressure placed on the three inside posts. It became necessary for us to create simple moves to reduce such strong internal pressure defense.

Most teams realize immediately the most effective way to restrict our efficient inside game is to concentrate on the denial of post passes. The nearness of the three post players makes it quite easy to run quick cuts or screens for each other. These moves reduce pressure while restoring more "honest" singular post coverage. They are listed below:

1. Cross Feed
2. Angling Back
3. Change

4. Change and Roll
5. Double Down

Each of these pressure breakers is described below in detail.

1. Cross Feed

The first of these forward pressure breakers is the Cross Feed, or angled post pass, as shown in Diagram 2-14. The handling guard 2 is not limited to feeding the post player who is positioned only on his own side. He can also feed directly to post 3 as well. This Cross Feed is best executed by using a bounce pass. This, then, forces single post defensive responsibility which makes future post feeding much easier. Once the guard cross feeds, the nonpassing guard runs his normal vision cut as if he had passed the ball. After 5 runs his crosscut, the Pass and Pick Attack is now set to go.

2. Angling Back

Guards who are average ball handlers can feed posts regardless of post defense. Dribbling to improve post feeding is called Angling

Back. The ball-handling guard (2 in Diagram 2-15) attempts to start the Pass and Pick Attack but finds his post fronted by X4. Player 2 then begins his vision cut while dribbling. This change in ball position forces X4 to adjust yet prevent himself from being sealed on 4's back. Once 2 passes to 4, after his angling move, he completes his vision cut to the baseline as 3 and 5 begin the Pass and Pick.

3. *Change*

High posts draw many defensive fouls by their defenders simply because it's an extremely difficult position to deny passes successfully. In their anxiety to get over the top and extend hands in the passing lane, they commit many body fouls even before the post pass is in the air. There is great pressure on this post defender who must get over, or under, the post as the ball is being dribbled outside him, yet within close passing range. The post simply stays in a broad stance while rotating his body to face the ball and offering appropriate hand targets.

After angling his vision cut, 2 may find himself still unable to hit post 4. Player 4's biggest role here is not to "beg" by waiting, but to screen away (or change) with post 3 as shown in Diagram 2-16. Seeing no immediate pass, 4 runs a headhunt screen for 3 (or simply exchanges with 3) who replaces him. Post 3 cuts either above or below 4's screen but must come to 4's spot for 2's pass. From a strategic viewpoint in actual competition, we permit only their straight change and replace during the game's first half. We hope to establish a defensive stereotype of this particular move, and then exploit it in

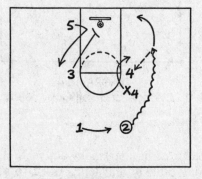

DIAGRAM 2-15
Angling Back

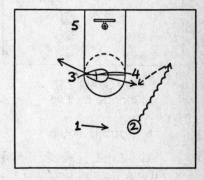

DIAGRAM 2-16
Change

the second half with the next pressure breaker. Post 3 is now able to run the Pass and Pick as 4 screens down for 5.

4. Change and Roll

The next pressure breaker, the Change and Roll, is shown in Diagrams 2-17 and 2-18. It is strictly a second-half tool in our games. Player 3's defender assumes that 4 will always change with 3 as he did in the first half, then remain there waiting to screen down for the Pass and Pick. Player X3 is sometimes lazy in establishing the proper helpside positioning with respect to 2, who has the ball. Upon contact with X3, 4 spins quickly (toward the ball, not the baseline) and rolls down the cleared-out lane looking for 2's direct pass. Player 5 helps clear out the low area by filling 3's vacated position. Player 2 looks for either 4 rolling low or to 3 who has flashed toward him.

Diagram 2-18 shows the completed cuts after a Change and Roll. Player 4, who rolls low, is not open and has crossed the lane filling for 5. Player 5, who empties the baseline for 4's roll move, fills 4's high spot; 3 is usually open on the near high post to begin the Pass and Pick again.

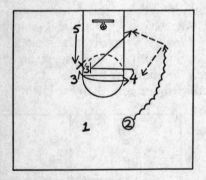

DIAGRAM 2-17
Change and Roll

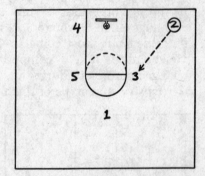

DIAGRAM 2-18
Change and Roll Completed

5. Double Down

The final pressure breaker for posts is extremely active and confusing for the defense. It develops quickly and lends itself to a special scoring play and a pressure release. This release, as well as others, requires no vocal signal to indicate what will be run. When the handling guard sees either one or both posts being fronted by their defenders, he picks up his dribble and holds the ball high with both hands overhead as if to attempt a two-handed lob pass. He cocks his wrists several times as if to throw the normal lob to any fronted post player. The nonhandling guard 2, seeing the pass fake, steps back behind the line of the ball to create a safety release for 1 if 1's defender swarms all over him looking for a five-second call. The faked lob pass signals the Double Down, as shown in Diagrams 2-19 and 2-20. Both posts then wheel around and cross each other while cutting to their opposite low-post areas. To eliminate any collision, the post whose guard signaled, cuts first. Post 3, heading away from 5 low, goes to the block, then flashes up the lane ending opposite his original post spot. Post 4, who is heading toward 5 low, sets a downscreen on 5's defender. Player 5 can either use this screen to flash up the lane on that same side to become the high post, or he can run a straight backdoor cut filling the other low post area. Post 4's route depends on 5's choice to go high or low. Post 4 will go opposite 5's cut.

Diagram 2-19 shows 5 coming high. Post 4, seeing this, stays low either for boards or the beginning of Pass and Pick.

Diagram 2-20 has 5 crossing to the other low-post position. Post 4, seeing 5's crossing move, flashes up high to fill opposite his original position. The ball is easily posted now and results in either a shot attempt or the Pass and Pick Attack.

These pressure breakers contribute great finishing touches to the 2-2-1 man offenses. The guards have freeing moves with the Dribble Cross, while the forwards have several simple pressure

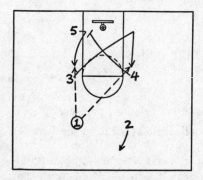

DIAGRAM 2-19
Double Down 5 High

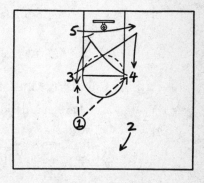

DIAGRAM 2-20
Double Down 5 Low

releases; all of which can serve equally well as quick, explosive scoring plays.

PROGRESSIVE MAN-OFFENSE TEACHING DRILLS

In order to teach an offense thoroughly, you must use the whole-part approach to learning. It's best to show this in its entirety first by multiple means, such as using returning players on the court, chalk-talks, mimeographed handouts, overhead projectors with overlays, or any available game films. Learning is hastened if a new item is explained on one day using one or more of these chosen methods, then actually doing the court work the following practice day.

Today's athletes want to know the "why" of everything they do, including drills. The whole-part style promotes understanding of each drill in the athlete's eyes after each offensive component is isolated and practiced. "Why," "how," and "coaching tips" are clearly and concisely stated for each drill.

All drills are limited to five minutes each. If the drill is still not learned sufficiently, it will be repeated later.

The order of drills is organized to develop total understanding. The Pass and Pick and the Dribble Cross are both taught progressively using only proven drills for each specific offense. The teaching completely covers the following areas, where applicable:

1. *Entry Drills*—getting the ball safely into the operational areas
2. *Pattern Drills*—actual offensive and shooting drills
3. *Counter Drills*—used to discourage defensive "cheating"

PASS AND PICK ENTRY DRILLS

Pop-Up Drill (Diagram 2-21)

WHY: 1. To have guards face a variety of defensive pressures.

HOW: 1. Two guards, each with a ball, begin at backcourt hash marks with defender's X1.

2. Guards advance by dribble versus X1's pressure until mid-court line. Guard X1 releases the guard; then X2, waiting at the hash mark, comes up hard to pressure guard again all the way until guard makes post pass to unguarded post at elbow.

3. Post returns ball to guard on his vision cut route and guard shoots the jumper.
4. Guards in backcourt begin same routine after the shots.
5. Guards switch sides of the court when shot is over.
6. Add defensive posts later.

TIPS:
1. Vary defender's pressure by having them do the following:
   a. Funnel to middle
   b. Fan to sideline
   c. Play the dribbler's weak hand
   d. Play them "straight up"
2. Allow two defenders at hash mark to both spring at dribbler for a double-team. Insist that guard backs away from the trap, keeping the dribble alive.
3. Rotate all players for dribbling and defensive work.
4. Have groups hold shooting competitions between guards.

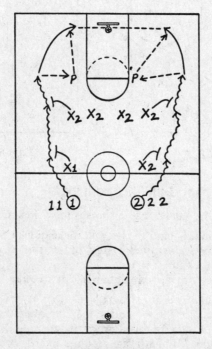

DIAGRAM 2-21

"X" Drill (Diagram 2-22)

WHY:
1. To direct guards' penetration.

HOW: 1. Place a large "X" on the court using two strips of gym tape
             each 12 feet long. Make the center of the "X" four feet wide of
             the lane and six feet from the top of the key.
          2. Guards try to penetrate versus defenders who pressure them
             away from the "X".

TIPS: 1. As guards improve, the coach snips off parts of the "X" tape
             creating a smaller "X" and making a smaller target for the
             guards to land on.
          2. Set a time limit on the "X" arrival for the guards. Then vary
             the guards' departure points.
          3. Vary defensive influence the same four ways as in the Pop-
             Up Drill.

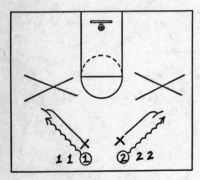

DIAGRAM 2-22

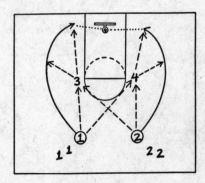

DIAGRAM 2-23

Vision Shooting Drill (Diagram 2-23)

WHY: 1. Give guards game shots from vision cut routes.

HOW: 1. Guards pass to post and make quick vision cuts.
          2. Posts give quick return passes to cutting guards for their
             quick jump shots.
          3. Vary by allowing guards' Cross Feeds.

TIPS: 1. Guards change court sides.
          2. Add defensive guards, then later add defensive posts.
          3. Use this drill as a pregame warm-up drill.
          4. Play "21" with one group of guards competing against the
             other.

Post Solo Drill (Diagram 2-24)

WHY: 1. Give posts practice using one-on-one over cleared-out side.

HOW: 1. Station guards at front and side positions.
2. Guards alternately feed the post on their side.
3. Post squares up facing the basket and reads the defender's positioning.
4. Post drives or shoots based on defender's distance.
5. Posts switch sides.
6. Run alternately on each side to avoid lane mishaps.

TIPS: 1. Add defensive guards using "up and back" defensive fakes on all passing guards.
2. Place a third guard on the baseline with a defender who may help on the post's drive. The post may drop the pass down to the baseline guard who shoots the jumper or drives the baseline.

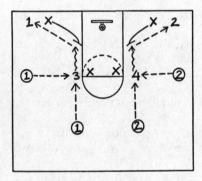

DIAGRAM 2-24

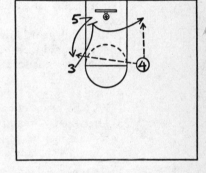

DIAGRAM 2-25

PASS AND PICK PATTERN DRILLS

Three-man Game Drill (Diagram 2-25)

WHY: 1. To teach the Pass and Pick Continuity.

HOW: 1. Post 4 starts with the ball as 3 sets downscreen on 5.
2. Run the Pass and Pick repeatedly with no guards—just the three posts.

TIPS: 1. Use no defense initially. Gradually add defenders one by one as the players' confidence develops.
2. Add the low post's backdoor option.
3. Give a minimum number of passes before a shot can be taken.

4. Give a maximum number of passes before a shot can be taken.
5. Designate the shooter and the shot location.
6. Put guards in the post rotation to develop their total perspective of the offense.
7. On all shot attempts insist on the strict coverage of the three rebounding triangle corners.

COUNTER DRILLS
FOR DRIBBLE CROSS CONTINUITY

CPR (Cross, Pick and Roll) Drill (Diagram 2-26)

WHY:
1. Practice guards' dribble exchange or cross movement.
2. Develop pick and roll skills for guards and forwards.

HOW:
1. Both guards are being pressed by respective defenders in the backcourt.
2. Handling guard 1 dribbles hard for opposite corner as 2 cuts in front and then hooks back to 1's line.
3. Post 4 sets his screen for 1 and they play pick and roll for a score.
4. Post 3 fights for inside offensive rebounding position against X3 who boxes out.
5. After the two-man play, 2 on the right side of the backcourt repeats the process of dribble exchange, pick and roll with P3, as P4 rebounds.

TIPS:
1. Have post defenders eventually jump in guard's path looking for the charge just before the post's backscreen.
2. Have a ten-basket game for posts to play against each other. Baskets count that are scored by posts or guards during the two-man play, in addition to those scored from missed shots and offensive rebounds.
3. Place a half-circle of gym tape on a radius 18 feet from the basket. The crossing guard must stay within the tape as his defender tries to influence him out of this 18-foot range. The defense scores two points every time they force the guard on or past the tape, get an offensive turnover, or get a defensive rebound. The offense scores one point for staying inside the tape and two points for each basket.

Cannibal Drill (Diagram 2-27)

WHY:
1. To teach 4 and 5 to work together quickly on the low screen.
2. To get players used to playing in the crowded low-post "physical" area.

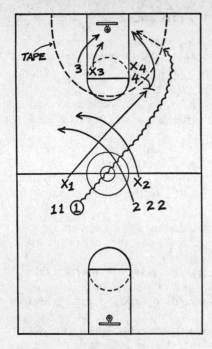

DIAGRAM 2-26

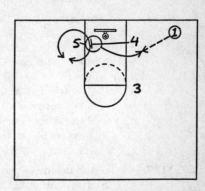

DIAGRAM 2-27

HOW:
1. Baseline guard 1 with the ball tries to pass to 4 in low post.
2. Player 4's post defender plays him any way he chooses.
3. Player 4 headhunts 5's lane defender as 5 cuts off the screen either high or low.
4. Player 4 briefly pops off the screen opposite 5's cut for a brief look at 1 with the ball. He then clears out of the lane away to the opposite low post.
5. Player 1 passes to whoever is open and the shot is immediately taken.

TIPS:
1. Add a defender to 1, but now he can also shoot or drive the baseline.
2. Give 3 a ball too and he passes to whomever 1 doesn't. This gives more shots for more people in a given time period.
3. Add a defender to 3, but now he can also shoot from his post spot.
4. Emphasize the title *Cannibal* to develop inside aggressiveness.

Swing and Go Drill (Diagrams 2-28A and 2-28B)

WHY:
1. To develop quickness of ball reversal.
2. To quicken 4's move up the lane for the two-man game.

HOW:
1. Baseline guard 1 reverses ball to 2 directly or via 3's relay pass.
2. After ball is reversed, 4 comes up for pick and roll with 2, but 4 can't leave until the ball is released from the baseline guard.
3. After the pick and roll shot is taken, the ball is sent out to 2 in the corner and 4 goes back to his high post.
4. Player 3 goes low on weak side as 1 comes high and the drill is reversed on the other side of the court, as shown in Diagram 2-28B.

TIPS:
1. Add defensive posts before adding defensive guards.
2. After adding defensive guards, allow the baseline guard to either shoot or drive the baseline.
3. Have a ten-basket game between players on the right sides of the lane against the players on the left side.
4. Switch guards and forwards to develop total offensive perspective.
5. Run 12 players in the drill using teams of 4 on a team. Rotate every ten ball possessions. Offense goes to the baseline, defense becomes the offense, and the baseline team becomes the defense. The winning team is the one who scores the most from their ten possessions. Offensive rebounds that result in scores count. Give some appropriate rewards for the winning team.

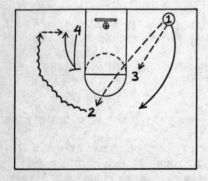

DIAGRAM 2-28A

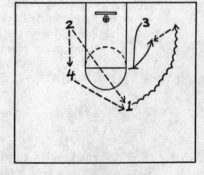

DIAGRAM 2-28B

CHAPTER 3:

Posting and Penetrating from the 2-2-1

Whether a team chooses to walk or run the ball upcourt, the fact remains that consistent scoring is always decided by the team with the strongest inside game. The defensive "heart" is located close to the basket. The team that attacks this heart creates many close-in shots that produce extra fouling. This opening premise cannot be overstated in this chapter's development.

In addition to getting the ball posted, winning basketball involves developing all players' one-on-one skills. This "mini-offense" within a team offense is also responsible for the outcome of many ball games. Although some of today's great players instinctively perform the right moves during a one-on-one confrontation, most do not and must be taught.

THREE HIGH-POST DEFENSIVE STYLES

There are three basic techniques used when defending the high post areas. We focus on the elbow high post and the defenses we've faced.

Side Front

Some defenders are taught to "side front" all high posts. They employ a standard hand-in-the-lane overplay or denying stance to discourage passes. Some defenders are quite talented at this as they've been drilled continually to deny a moving forward in the wing or baseline areas. The transition to a stationary player on a post is a less tiring task following this active practice.

Behind

Other defensive posts are taught to play one step behind the high post without the ball. The theory of this technique is based on the post's inability to score after catching the ball until he squares up to face the basket. Then the defender steps up to apply pressure. This "play-behind" defense is commonly used by a defensive post who is much larger and possibly slower than the offensive post. This style of play allows the defender to use his strength and size to a better advantage than if he tried to match agility by playing a denial defensive stance. This defender is taught to make no contact during the post pass. This gives no indication to the post where his defender is positioned. He now must totally square up to the basket to locate his defender and begin an offensive move.

Straight Front

The third style of high post defense is rarely used but has, on occasion, successfully stopped a good post-passing attack. This approach focuses on the defender fronting the post and inviting the lob pass. This method is adapted from the 1-3-1 standard zone defense. The defensive point in the standard zone defense is instructed to front the middle high post aggressively, especially if there is a nonscoring offensive point guard. The "straight front" defense is often an effective method when the defender is quick with good jumping ability. The quick jump successfully stops the encouraged lob pass. If a team has strong helpside defense it is likely to defend a strong high post with the straight front. An added benefit to this method is realized during later stages of the game when a frustrated post begins pushing off on the attempted lob pass and starts accumulating fouls.

The three approaches to high-post defense in the elbow areas are shown in Diagram 3-1.

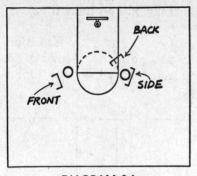

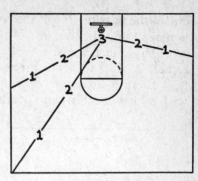

DIAGRAM 3-1
High Post Defenses

DIAGRAM 3-2
Line of Three

LINE OF THREE

It is vital that the guards line themselves up properly with the post player and the basket. The guard's ability to dribble toward this line when under great defensive pressure will lead to many completed post passes. Whether the post is located on the high elbow, side post, or the low post, it is imperative that the guard place himself on this proper line. This line of the guard, post, and basket is called the *line of three*. This term is easily understood and serves as a strong visual idea as to what we need to initiate our attack. The line of three is shown in Diagram 3-2. Player 1 is the passing guard, 2 is the post on the lane, and 3 is the basket itself.

The guard's strongest weapon when aligning himself properly is the crossover dribble. This allows good straight-ahead vision and enables him to deliver the ball during any split-second defensive lapses. Passing opportunities last but a second and must be exploited immediately. We stress repeatedly to our guards the need to fake through the different passing "holes" first and then pass the ball accurately to the post.

Diagram 3-3 is a chart to record the number of times each guard successfully enters the ball into the post during games.

If the pass is completed, a straight line is drawn from the numbered guard's exact court position to the post's position. This line depicts the attempted pass, so you can analyze its success or failure based on the line of three principle. If the pass is completed, the straight line is left untouched. If the post pass is not completed, a short line is slashed at that point where it was deflected or stolen. If the defensive guard deflects the ball, the slash is placed on the guard's end of the passing line. If the ball is lost at the post position, the slash is placed on the other end of the passing line.

This chart is easily kept and reveals a lot about a team's inside attack. It pinpoints the number of times post passes are thrown, who tries them, who can feed the post best and from which side, along with a host of additional posting data.

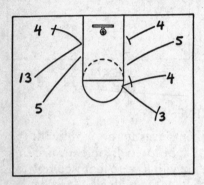

DIAGRAM 3-3
Posting Chart

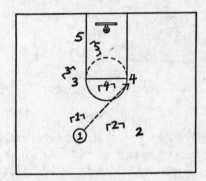

DIAGRAM 3-4
Guard-Weak Post

ANGLED POST PASSES

The exception to the line of three passing principle occurs when both of the high posts are occupied and the two guards are parallel and wider than the lane's width.

Each guard has a great passing angle to hit the weakside post player, if that post's defender is sagging to help deny the strongside post pass.

Diagram 3-4 shows defender ⌞ 4 ⌟ sagging off his post 4 to stop guard 1's pass into strongside post 3. This "cheating" position opens up two distinct post passes.

Two Angled Post Passes

1. Guard-Weak Post
2. Guard-Guard-Weak Post

Guard-Weak Post

The first post option is guard 1's diagonal pass. This is available when weakside post defender ⌞ 4 ⌟ sags toward the ball and the guard's defender ⌞ 2 ⌟ plays up in the guard-guard passing lane. Remember, however, that defender ⌞ 4 ⌟ is not likely to sag too far from 4 because of two reasons. First, 4 is in good shooting range if a pass should get through to him. Second, the highly potent Pass and Pick man attack with 4's quick downscreen also tends to keep ⌞ 4 ⌟ close to home. See Diagram 3-4.

Guard-Guard-Weak Post

Should 2's defender ⌞ 2 ⌟ also sag to help deny either the 1-3 or 1-4 post passes, then the guard to guard pass is automatic. This is shown in Diagram 3-5. Following this pass from guard 1 to guard 2, a quick dribble will easily free 4 for 2's pass. This can lead to an immediate one-on-one move, a set play, or a pattern.

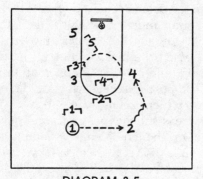

DIAGRAM 3-5

TARGET HANDS

The posting game's efficiency is reduced if there is not a strong communication between the post and his feeding guard. The post must constantly use his *away* hand as a silent indicator to the passing guard. The away hand is that hand furthest from the defender. This properly positioned hand can designate just where the post feels he can best receive the ball and also implies that he is in control of his defender. *Control of the defender* means that the post knows both where his defender is and that he can score on him if he gets the ball. The post has created his own passing lane if the guard can see a flat palm that is facing him.

The hand, itself, must be positioned so that there is no guess-work where he wants the ball. The thumb must stay at right angles to the forearm, with the four fingers pointing in the direction of the desired pass. Our guards are taught to pass away from the defensive player and not to the offensive target hand. This forces the post player to reach an extra few inches for the pass but helps to eliminate a steal or deflection.

POST SEALING

If a post defender actively tries to deny the pass to the high post, we teach a sealing maneuver. This seal move is adjustable to any of the 2-2-1's designated posting areas, but it is especially valuable up high as there is much less immediate defensive help there than down in the low-post area.

The defender takes his strong denial position on either side of the post man. Once the defensive post begins to establish his overplay position, the post man must move with him. The offensive post's sliding steps directly follow the defender's moves that are used while denying the pass. When the defense moves, the offense must move immediately. Strong and choppy steps maintain a strong pass-receiving stance. The post's maneuvering for the ball takes place on an imaginary arc, which keeps him close to the lane. Several imaginary posting areas and foot positions are shown in Diagram 3-6. The arcs are shown on the left side of the lane.

The post must use slide steps beginning with the foot nearest his defender and step toward the ball while putting his back to the defender. It is vital that the foot nearest the defense be at least even to, and preferably in front of, the defender's leading foot.

This position turns the post slightly away and drops his center of gravity down low for better balance and body control. The back hand then becomes the target hand and is extended away from the body to signal passing direction and control.

The seal move, including the proper foot alignment, is shown on the right elbow of the court in Diagram 3-6. The post, feeling strong pressure on his left, slides his left foot up to line up with the ball. This creates a three-point imaginary line starting with the right foot, then the post's left foot, and finally the ball. The guard again passes away from defender ⌞ 4 ⌟ to a point just beyond the post's back target hand.

Once the pass is posted against a sealed defender, a one-on-one, set play, or pattern can be run effectively. The major goal of getting the ball inside has been achieved, and it will pay dividends.

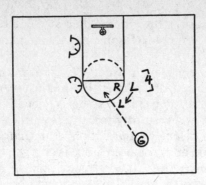

DIAGRAM 3-6

RECEIVING POST PASSES

Strong hand and arm position can aid a post in catching passes. It is important to locate the direction of any defensive pressure, so that no surprise steals or deflections occur. The easiest way to determine pressure is for the post to raise his arms so that the elbows are shoulder level with the hands being tilted slightly inward as if to receive a pass. This becomes an obvious passing invitation and forces the defender to reveal his planned style of defensive positioning. Once known, the proper sealing techniques can be used.

The defensive post may play slightly off the post's back and not commit himself to denying a side. In this event, the post can't casually believe that his defender will not move up for the steal or deflection. As the pass is thrown, the post must extend his arms directly in front and catch the ball a full arm's distance away. This effectively shortens the passing lane and reduces the defender's chances. After this pass is caught, the ball must be brought quickly to a point under the chin with the elbows flared outward.

TEACHING ONE-ON-ONE PLAY

Coaching relies strongly on building a strong coach-player relationship. Players are full of questions that center on the "why" of each explanation. One of the best ways to develop this strong rapport is to personalize your teaching by stressing individual one-on-one moves. Because of television's constant focus on only the ball and its temporary handler, there is a powerful desire in each player to excel in this popular phase of the game. When an athlete feels a coach has converged on just him to teach some moves, the player usually listens attentively.

Although some players instinctively perform the proper move in a one-on-one situation, most must be taught several maneuvers to enhance their game. Players must be coached on how to read a defensive position and instantly react to it with the proper offensive thrust. Reading a defensive foundation is an undeveloped talent. It must be understood and mastered if one is going to become proficient with the ball. Many players have already predetermined their move even before catching the ball. This is thought-out regardless of the defense's position. Such a practice leads to many offensive charges, violations, or at least a poor shot attempt. Players must be taught to recognize and not to predetermine. This reading skill builds a player's confidence; he knows he has the first attacking move.

One-on-one skills are best learned during the first half of practice sessions when the players are fresher and more receptive to individual work. They should practice only "game shots from game spots at game speeds." Fancy shots don't impress me as a coach. Degree of difficulty doesn't count—only that the scoreboard goes "click-click!"

The dribble must be used sparingly in the "solo" game. We stress that a player's first two dribbles are to earn *him* a shot. After the second dribble, his objective had better be to earn *someone else* a shot. The one-on-one game can be injurious to the team concept, and limited dribbling is good coach control.

All players must also be taught their shooting range and quick execution of all moves. Each shot must be delivered from good body balance and with confidence. Teammates must be able to anticipate the shooter's release of the ball so that they can cover the likely offensive rebounding areas. They must also be able to become available as pass receivers, should their man drop off to stop the one-on-one effort.

During 2-on-2 or 3-on-3 half-court games, a special effort must be made to use the learned moves from the 2-2-1's basic areas. Players must be taught *when* to fake. Faking a 30-foot jump shot is as unrealistic as an attempted drive into a packed zone. Fakes must also be kept simple, quick, and not overexaggerated.

Potential shooters must also be reminded to get an "early look" at the basket. If the ball handler looks down, he has lost visual sight of the basket for a few seconds. This is comparable to teaching the baseball pitcher to maintain eye contact with the catcher's glove during the pitcher's wind-up. A shooter's task in relocating the basket while heavily defended is very difficult.

A sound one-on-one player must develop the following skills to be totally effective:

1. Pass or make lay-ups off the dribble. The "wrong foot" lay-up must be mastered.

2. Drive well with either hand.

3. Have a medium range jumper following a pivot.

4. Pull up off the dribble for the jumper. The charge must be avoided.

HIGH POST ONE-ON-ONE PLAY

Both high and low posts, after receiving the ball, must understand the order of their options. The high post must, in order: (1) pass, (2) shoot, and then (3) drive. This sequence differs when the ball is posted low, and this will be discussed shortly.

When operating from the high post or elbow, as in the 2-2-1 set, it is crucial that the ballplayer understand his role. The ball had been posted to him at the elbow when the passing guard felt he was open and could score quickly. The one-on-one play from this popular 15-foot position is best understood when broken down into the following three areas:

1. The Facing Pivot

2. The Read

3. The Moves

During the description of these three phases there is an attempt to describe completely each of the teaching quotes we use that best illustrates, in the players' minds, the basic desired action.

The Facing Pivot

There are two types of pivots used after receiving the ball at the elbow. One occurs naturally when there is no apparent pressure. The other pivot is done automatically following an attempted steal or strong defensive pressure. These pivots are called the natural pivot and the pressure pivot.

Natural pivot. If a player feels no defender leaning into him during the post pass, he pivots and "faces up," based on his dominant hand. We rely on the most comfortable foot that players naturally use if there are no other instructions given. If a player is right-handed, his best pivot foot is his left foot. This gives him his best side from which to begin his moves. The opposite applies to a lefty; his right foot serves as the strongest pivoting side. This natural pivot is one the players will execute with confidence. Subsequent moves following this pivot are taught more easily if a player is comfortable and can begin his move with his strong foot.

The natural pivot is done whether the post is on the left or right side of the free throw line. When both posts pivot on the natural opposite foot, as described, one will be on the foul line itself and the other will be slightly on the foul line extended. This may appear to be an unfamiliar operating position, but I feel the natural comfort derived from the opposite foot serving as the pivot foot far outweighs the three-foot lateral difference in foot positioning. This is shown in Diagram 3-7. Each post is right-handed and pivots on his left foot during his "face-up" move. The pivot foot is circled.

The term "face-up" is used for its multiple uses. It is used as a noun as a labeled move and also serves as a coaching verb. The term "face-up" is currently used when our players encounter tough life problems and responsibilities to be dealt with. This term has great carry-on value when we discuss other parts of their lives. Familiarity of terms eases player understanding.

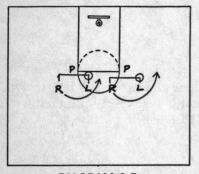

DIAGRAM 3-7

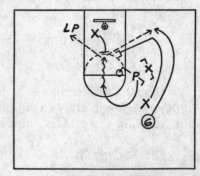

DIAGRAM 3-8

Pressure pivot. The second pivot from the elbow position is dictated by the defense. If the post defender either attempts a steal of the post pass or leans on the post while declaring a denial side, the pressure pivot is used. This is a natural act that we drill on to prepare a player to attack the defender's exposed side. The foot which is opposite the defender's quickly applied pressure is the designated pivot foot. This quick pivot is often followed by an immediate drive to the basket past the overly-committed defender. There must be special thought given to dropping the ball off low to either a baseline guard or the low post if their defenders rush up to stop the immediate scoring threat. This pressure pivot off an attempted steal is shown in Diagram 3-8.

The post, feeling defender X's pressure on his left side, pivots on his right foot after receiving guard G's pass. Following the pivot, the post drives the lane looking to score after one or two dribbles. He then hits the open low post or the dropped baseline guard G, if either of their defenders helps stop the ball's penetration.

Both pivots must be demonstrated and repeatedly drilled. Coaches must not assume that their players know how to pivot properly—they must be taught! Both the natural and the pressure pivot are strong habits to develop as they are very instinctive in nature and not awkward for most players. Each serves as strong building blocks for ensuing scoring moves.

The ball, during both pivots, must be placed in a strong operating position. The hands should be adjusted on the ball so that either the shot or the dribble can be executed without further repositioning. The player's dominant hand should be on top of the ball at a "12" o'clock position and the remaining hand should be at either the "3" or "9" spots, based on which hand is the "guide" hand. It is vital to receive the ball with the hands quickly on these "clock spots" for instant execution.

The Read

The "reading" of the nearest post defender directly follows the facing pivot. Each player must first look to pass the ball either to the low post or to a baseline guard on the ball side. If neither player is open, the post must determine how *he* is being defended. There are basically three positions a defender can use:

1. Overplaying right or left.
2. Playing off more than an arm's length.
3. Playing up close to the shooter.

The Countering Moves

Each of these defensive positions has a definite offensive move to counter:

Overplaying right or left. When a defender eliminates either one of the two driving lanes, the other becomes vulnerable to a quick drive.

This drive is best done if it is preceded by a fake toward the defender's strong side. Such a fake tends to "freeze" the defender momentarily or may even get him leaning in that direction.

The fake is executed by stepping toward the defender's strength, using the free foot as the attacking weapon. The free foot does not touch the floor but it is returned quickly in a long step toward the baseline as the first dribble begins. The second step is done with the original pivot foot. It is placed as near as possible to the defender's outside foot. The angle of the drive is toward the baseline. This baseline route is very important, as some drivers head toward the sideline in an effort to avoid the defender and end up taking the wider sideline route. This allows the defender time to recover. As soon as the drive begins, the defender must execute a drop-step with his up foot and shift his weight to contend with the driver. The dribbler then places his head as close to the defender's hip as possible and tries to get the inside shoulder by.

Once the shoulder gets by the defender, the dribbler tries to "close the door" on his man. This is done by pushing off on the outside foot and angling the body in front of the retreating defender. Such a move impedes the defender's retreating movements and may cause a foul. These movements and teaching principles are shown in Diagram 3-9.

Playing off further than an arm's length. This defensive positioning is often used in the 2-2-1 attack as players try to use up and back fakes while trying to help jam the passing lanes. This movement opens up the 15-foot jump shot. This shot is familiar because the distance and visual background are similar to the free throw. This shot is especially open when the defender has his feet parallel and his hands are down. This stance limits a defender's forward attacking

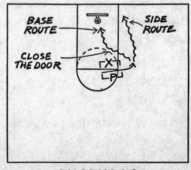

DIAGRAM 3-9

ability while jumping. A person can jump forward higher and with more control if he does so from a staggered stance rather than from a parallel stance. This position also lends itself to follow through fouls.

A second choice is to dribble directly toward the backed-off defender. His normal reaction is to use a short retreat step. This tilts his body weight slightly backwards, making it tough to respond to the post's short jumper following the attacking dribble.

Playing up. If a post defender chooses to play the ball tightly, the post must instantly read the defender's up foot. Defenders often swarm the post to block passing vision of the Penetration's short passing lanes. The defender is now susceptible to a quick one-on-one drive through a cleared-out side. This up foot is the defender's weak side, as discussed earlier, and it must be attacked aggressively. The teaching principles of sideline route, baseline route, and closing the door are again drilled repeatedly.

LOW-POST PRESSURE MOVES

The term *low post* means many things to many players and coaches. From a teaching standpoint, it is best to eliminate any vagueness and precisely delineate this area. We define the low post as that area between the block and the next lane marker. This provides our players a precise spot that is labeled by consistent floor markings. The primary advantage of this area is that it gives a longer baseline area down the lane in which to play the power game.

This low post is the game's premier scoring area, but with this increased accuracy goes escalated defensive pressure. Most coaches spend practice time daily to stress the strength and agility need to defend the talented low-post scorer.

There are three styles of defending the low post. The offensive player must have experience facing all of them to be a consistent scorer. The standard low-post defensive techniques are as follows:

1. Straight Front
2. Top Side
3. Bottom Side

The low player must learn to handle this constant leaning pressure by using positional adjustments. These pressure releases will easily free the low post for good passes.

Straight Front

When a low post is being straight fronted, there is a direct line between the defender, the post, and the basket. The post can respond in either of the following two ways.

1. Up move. First, he can move up the lane toward the elbow. This move has now broadened the area in the lane for a lob pass.

After following the move up the lane, the post must then "locate" the defender by placing his sideline elbow in the small of the back of the fronting defender. The other hand serves as an active, signaling target hand for the expectant lob pass. This target hand again indicates the post's control of the defender and is an unspoken signal for the lob. When the lob is released, the post must maintain contact with the elbow until the pass is directly over the post's head. We teach the extended elbow as a locater rather than the forearm, so our post won't be tempted to push off the defender during the lob attempt. The guard lobs toward the board's near corner.

2. Cross move. The second style of combating the straight front is by crossing the lane and catching a weakside swing pass with the defender being contained on the post's back. This containment is best executed if the post, when crossing the lane, keeps his elbows at shoulder height and hands up as if he were boxing out. The fronting post defender is considered a part of a zone defense and the normal zone approach of the weakside swing is signaled by the post pointing to the weakside. The guard with the ball, seeing this pointing, reverses the ball directly or by skip-passing as the post crosses the lane. The post can be hit either on the way across the lane or he can receive the ball on the opposite low post from a popped-out forward. It is imperative when receiving the ball that the post lands using a two-foot jump stop. This enables him to use either foot as a pivot foot while pivoting to face up and begin an offensive maneuver.

Both the up and cross moves are shown in Diagrams 3-10 and 3-11.

Top Side

Occasionally, a defender may position himself above the post and up the lane in an attempt to deny a post pass. Either one or both of the following moves will easily free the post.

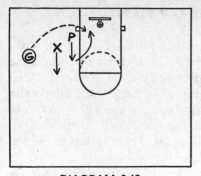

DIAGRAM 3-10
Up Move

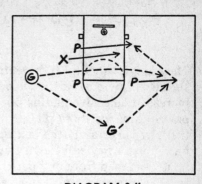

DIAGRAM 3-11
Cross Move

1. *Post seal—guard dribble—bounce pass.* The post will seal his man (as described earlier) as the guard dribbles toward the baseline to improve his passing angle. This is best followed by a bounce pass to the dropping post and will result in a good shot. This series is shown in Diagram 3-12.

2. *Up move.* This move up the lane, as discussed when faced with a straight front, is again used to expand the available lob-pass area.

Bottom Side

A defender may attempt to take away a low post's best hand by playing him to the side and from the direction of the baseline. When a post sees this defensive stance, he leans into the pressure toward the baseline and executes a sealing move. This will open up a wider passing lane and reduce the defender's chances at deflections.

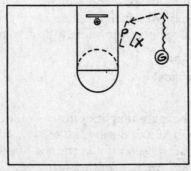

DIAGRAM 3-12

LOW POST ONE-ON-ONE PLAY

The low post has its order of options after receiving the ball. They are: (1) shoot, (2) drive, and (3) pass. The stress placed on the shot first obviously depends on the proximity of the basket and the increased defensive fouling opportunities. The drive itself allows the power game for those players who may lack finesse. The pass out of the lane is certainly the last option we want to exercise as we work hard to get the ball down low. We'll get it out only when we are double-teamed from any perimeter defenders.

The low post must have an awareness of where his defender is located before an aggressive move is attempted. This defensive location is accomplished two ways. The first is before the pass and the second is after the pass.

Defensive contact. The quickest method of finding the defender is both the most common and the easiest to react to. The defender's body is usually leaning on the post from either side or from straight in back. This lean is an immediate signal to the post that he should use a move designed to immediately counter the defensive position.

After the pass. If the post received a low pass, such as a bounce pass, he bends at the waist looking behind him for his opponent's sneakers. This tells the post if he is being defended from the top, baseline, off, or up tight.

If the ball is received at chest height or higher, the post quickly looks over his baseline shoulder to find the defender. This look may serve a dual role in that it can lean the defender in that same direction by making him think that a move is coming that way.

Our approach to low-post shooting may be a bit unorthodox but it has served us well. We teach different shots based on the players' strengths. Our basic shots from the low-post position are as follows:

1. Lane Hook Shot
2. Pump and Jump Shot
3. Bully Shot

These three shots are taught exclusively for all players who may find themselves posted low during the season. A player is allowed to use his strong hand in shooting certain shots during his first two years in our program. We realize that using both hands equally is the accepted style of teaching, but we want these shots perfected first with the strong hand. The junior year brings with it added confidence, coordination, and a firm muscle memory of the three shots. The players also realize that in the summer preceding their junior season they are to develop their weak hand when using these shots.

A description of these potent shots so vital in the 2-2-1 offense follows.

1. Lane Hook

I am a strong believer in our low post shooters *never* taking any shot that will carry them away from the basket. There are many lost rebounds that a shooter can't reach simply because his follow-through is a fade-away and this removes him from rebounding range. For this reason, we shoot the lane hook only in the lane and never down the lane line. This is why we call it the *lane hook*; so it serves as a constant reminder where it should be shot. Hook *into* the lane, not *down* the lane!

When defensive pressure is applied from the baseline, that is the signal for the lane hook. It is started with a double movement of the leg and arm nearest the free throw line. The leg is swung in the direction of the opposite low-post spot with a long, quick stride. This keeps the shot close and consistent while controlling the defender. It also keeps him slightly further away from any collapsing helpside players.

The corresponding arm is swung with the leg at the same angle. The elbow, not the hand, leads the way. When the hand is thrown first there is a natural tendency for the shooter to push off with the extended forearm. The elbow acts as a fulcrum upon which the shooter spins off should the defender attack the shooter. During the release of the lane hook the elbow is brought inward near the shooter's body. This eliminates any offensive push-off and allows the defender free access to the shooter. The ball, by that time, has been released. This withdrawal of the elbow may also create a body foul from the defender.

The wrist supplies the final impetus of the lane hook. The ball finally rolls off the middle finger with a backspin. Proper follow-through means a momentary wave "goodbye" to the ball. The shot is not banked but is aimed to go directly in. The shooter's release places him in the middle of the lane and ready for the offensive rebound.

2. Pump and Jump Shot

This shot is executed following a pivot toward the baseline and is triggered by the defender playing off the low post. Following the baseline pivot, the post brings the ball up into shooting position for a bank shot. If the defender doesn't attack to stop the shot, the shot is released. If the defender steps forward and rises to block the shot, the ball is dropped down from the pump fake and then quickly raised for its release. This shot is taught from both the right and left low posts regardless of a player's dominant hand.

3. Bully Shot

The bully shot is used when the defender is located either straight back or slightly on the top side. The low post is one dribble from the basket. The bully move is executed by first making a long, quick step toward the basket with the baseline leg. This effectively seals the post defender on the shooter's back. The dribble is really taught as a *bounce* rather than as a *dribble*. It is executed with not one, but *two* hands. Two hands are used for two important reasons. First, the shooter can get the "early look" at the basket during the drop-step, as no real skill is needed to take a low bounce with the ball without looking at it. The early look is one of the most overlooked fundamentals when teaching any type of shot. Second, the two-handed bounce places both hands firmly on the ball before and after the bounce. When the shooter begins the upward phase of his bully move, he'll get heavy defensive resistance and it will become readily apparent why both hands are needed.

The guide (nonshooting) hand is kept on the ball during the basket attack and is removed only at the last second during the ball's release. When a defender contacts or grabs the nonshooting hand, it must in no way interfere with the shot's delivery.

The term *bully* is both a noun and a verb, as I continue to teach this game using action terms. This is the only instance when we encourage our players to force a shot. It is no time for grace and soft, delicate form. It's a forced bully shot and is called just that.

To review, our lane hook is used during the first two years only by the player's strong hand. The right-handed player shoots the lane hook only when on the offensive left low post. The opposite applies to the left-handed post player. This builds confidence for this shot and enhances its learning during the last two years.

The pump and jump shot is taught from both sides but only with the strong hand. The strong hand only is used for all four years.

The bully shot is taught with the strong hand during the first two years, but the weak hand's development is encouraged during the last two years.

PROGRESSIVE ONE-ON-ONE
AND POSTING DRILLS

Warm-ups

Floor practice begins with a one-minute meeting at the center circle with two brief statements. The first indicates the major emphasis for the day. Examples are: (1) "Work for the great shot"; (2) "No backcourt turnovers"; (3) "Get as many second shots as possible"; and (4) "No reaching fouls."

Second, a thought on "life through basketball" is mentioned. An example may be the need to compliment each teammate at least once in practice. These points of emphasis vary each day so the coach can make a preseason list and follow it. Players love to learn such life principles and may relate to them later (often when the coach least expects it).

An alternative is to have the "IQ Test." I call the players up one by one to ask them either a basketball question or some type of basic current events question. They are split into two groups based on the accuracy of their answers. If a majority get the answer right, we play our warm-up music during the upcoming rope-jumping session that we begin each practice with. If most of them answer incorrectly, we play no music that day.

Following this, the players back off in a circle and pick up their jump ropes. During the early season I have the players face outward so they can't see each other make mistakes and laugh. After skills improve I turn them around. The manager then turns on the normal pregame warm-up music while the players jump rope to it.

Find the Line Drill (Diagram 3-13)

WHY: 1. Posts' lane slides and armwork
            2. Guards' dribbling, court vision, and line of three concept
            3. Posts' target hand signaling, pivots, and shooting

HOW: 1. Guards line up at half-court line; each has a basketball.
            2. Two posts are positioned at each elbow. Waiting posts form lines at the top of the key.
            3. Guards dribble toward the baseline as posts move up and down their respective lanes. They change positions often to move their guards on the line of three. Guards may have to "side dribble" back over their routes to stay on the line of three.

4. When post wants the ball he signals with his target hand for the ball.
5. Post then uses a shot designated by the coach.
6. Guards and posts each change sides of the court.

TIPS:
1. Vary by first adding a defensive guard and then a defensive post.
2. Coaches check posts' target hands and proper shot.
3. Switch baskets every other day so players will feel equally comfortable on both ends of the court.
4. When defensive posts are added, the post must use either of the two facing pivots, read the defense, and score.

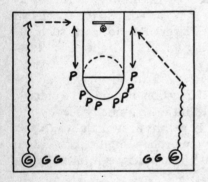 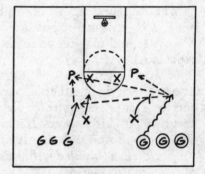

DIAGRAM 3-13   DIAGRAM 3-14

Angle and Seal Drill (Diagram 3-14)

WHY:
1. Angled passing to posts
2. Post sealing
3. One-on-one scoring moves
4. Facing pivots and reading the defenders

HOW:
1. Each guard on right side has a ball.
2. Defenders are assigned to both guards and posts.
3. Right guard dribbles from half court with defender X guarding him. Left guard advances level with the ball against his defender.
4. Defensive posts try to deny post passes.
5. Guards try to pass to (1) strong post, (2) weak post, or (3) other guard who then enters the ball to either post.
6. Once the ball is entered the post must read his defender and go one-on-one to score.
7. Passing guards become defensive guards; defensive posts

become offensive posts; offensive posts go to baseline to wait their turn.

TIPS: 1. Send the ball down both sides of the court.
        2. Have a competitive game. The guard who completes the pass to a post, and the post, each receive a point if the post scores on his defender. Winners (five points each position) get to skip a sprint drill or some comparable reward.

Three-man One-on-One Drill (Diagram 3-15)

WHY: 1. Posts' sealing and armwork techniques
        2. One-on-one scoring moves from both elbow and low-post areas
        3. Release pass out of pressure

HOW: 1. Guard G with ball tries to feed post P, who works legs and arms to get the pass. Post P can go to any elbow or low post.
        2. Defender X tries to deny all passes.
        3. Post P tries to score but releases to G if he doesn't have a good shot. P is allowed to release only twice to G before taking a shot.
        4. If post doesn't score, all three players rotate their positions in a clockwise direction. P becomes G, G becomes X, and X becomes P. If post does score, all three players stay and resume the drill.
        5. Game ends when one of the three players scores five baskets.
        6. On a defensive rebound, X becomes P and G stays.

TIPS: 1. Stress that P, after releasing to G, must immediately seal to get the ball right back.
        2. Insert new people into all positions. A great posting guard may emerge.

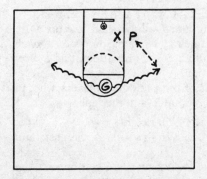

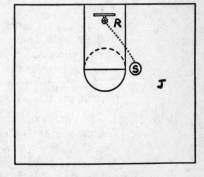

DIAGRAM 3-15   DIAGRAM 3-16

Skip and Shoot Drill (Diagram 3-16)

WHY: 1. Pressure jump shots when fatigued
               2. Coordination from jumping rope

HOW: 1. Three players: R=rebounder/feeder; S=jump shooter from elbow; J=player jumping rope.
               2. Shooter S takes ten elbow jumpers, keeping count of made shots. Rebounder feeds S as J keeps jumping rope.
               3. After ten shots, the jumper becomes the shooter as the shooter becomes the rebounder. The rebounder takes J's rope and begins jumping when the new S begins shooting.
               4. The player with the most made shots out of 30 attempts wins the drill.

TIPS: 1. Don't have the same players combine together each day. Have them change partners and baskets often.
               2. Keep a chart of the winners and play them off against each other as the season progresses.

Running the Eight Drill (Diagram 3-17)

WHY: 1. Post mobility and target hand development
               2. Rebounding and outlet passing
               3. One-on-one moves

HOW: 1. Four post players (1,2,3,4) begin at both elbows and low posts.
               2. Four guards (G) are positioned. Two are on the baseline and two are at the normal guard spots. All guards have a ball.
               3. Three rebounders (R) are positioned in the lane to retrieve all made or missed shots and then outlet the balls quickly to either of the two outlet players (0) positioned at the free throw line extended.
               4. Players 1, 2, 3, and 4 start following a figure-eight pattern touching all four posting areas (elbows and low posts) in their route. They must come to a two-foot jump stop at each spot and catch a pass from a guard and attempt an appropriate shot for that position.
               5. The guards receive passes from the outlet players who, in turn, got them from the rebounders in the lane.

TIPS: 1. Reverse the direction of the figure eight.
               2. Change guards and outlet players as well as the posts and rebounders.
               3. If a post doesn't get a pass from a guard, he continues to the next post spot, looking for a guard's pass and a shot.

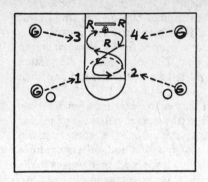

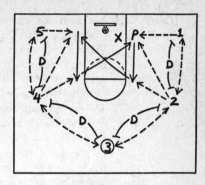

DIAGRAM 3-17   DIAGRAM 3-18

One-on-One Shell Drill (Diagram 3-18)

WHY: 1. Post passing under pressure
   2. One-on-one moves
   3. Defensive post denial skills

HOW: 1. Players 1,2,3,4 and 5 are stationary offensive players on the perimeter. P is the post moving to all four 2-2-1 posting areas.
   2. X defends P. The remaining Ds are also on the perimeter.
   3. Player 3 starts with the ball and can pass to any other perimeter player in addition to post P. Ds can't interfere with any perimeter passes.
   4. Ds can rush any perimeter player as long as he has the ball but must stay on this perimeter both *before* and *after* any pass. They can double-team only on players 2, 3, and 4 but must have single coverage on 1 and 5. This places extreme pressure on the passer.
   5. P goes one-on-one versus defender X when he gets the pass.

TIPS: 1. Change by having 1,2,3,4 and 5 switch with all Ds and X.
   2. On a defensive rebound, X and P switch roles.
   3. Keep score between both groups. The group that gets ten baskets first, wins. Losers must give a one-lap piggyback ride to each of the winners.

21 Solo Shot Drill (Diagram 3-19)

WHY: 1. Quickness in shot delivery
   2. Focus on specific shots
   3. Rebounding and outlet passing
   4. Fun and very competitive

HOW: 1. "As" and "Bs" are on opposite sides of the lane. One player from each team begins on their respective low posts.

2. The first player on each team (nearest the baseline) passes to his teammate on the low post. Low post takes a designated shot (coach-controlled) and follows it to rebound and then outlets it to the *last* person in his line.

3. The original shooter then flashes to elbow for a second pass from the last player in line (the one he just passed to). He then takes a second designated shot. The shooter again follows his shot as quickly as possible and outlets again to the last person in his lane. This last player then passes to the *second* player in line. The first passer is now in the low post. The original shooter then goes to the end of the line. The new front passer now passes into his teammate in the low post and the drill continues.

4. Each basket counts 1 point; 21 points wins the game.

TIPS: 1. Change sides of the floor for each team.

2. Use different baskets each day and mix up the teams.

3. Coach designates the shots to be taken. Examples: low (bully) high (jumper); low (lane hook) high (drive); low (pump and jump) high (crossover and drive).

4. Place four chairs in the four posting areas to serve as defenders. This develops offensive rebounding skills.

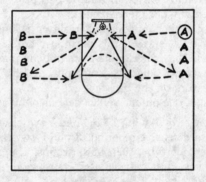

DIAGRAM 3-19

COACHING GUIDELINES FOR
POSTING AND ONE-ON-ONE PLAY

1. Have the first sub in for the post read the defensive post's style in the game, so he'll be well-prepared and able to help his teammate.

2. Posts must exert authority and show who is boss. A post is not measured by his height but by his heart.

3. A shooter's field-goal percentage is related to his refusal to take bad shots.

4. Develop your post's pass-catching abilities by purposely throwing him bad passes as well as good passes in practice. Vary the speeds of the passes to develop his hands. Experiment with throwing him different-sized athletic balls to force him to have strong eye contact with each pass thrown. He must "see the ball" into his hands.

5. Post practice is best done early in practice sessions when concentration is at its best.

6. The post must communicate with "hand talk."

7. What the defensive player does determines what the offensive player does.

8. Players must always be working very hard to catch the ball in their effective scoring ranges.

9. Once a defender is beaten, it is important that the driver "close the door" by taking up the defender's line of recovery to the basket.

10. Constant work on mobility must be done with all players as it is one of the most needed skills in basketball.

CHAPTER 4:

Using Three Guards with the Cross Lane Continuity Vs. All Zones

Many coaches begin each season with an oversupply of guards and just a handful of inside players. The resourceful coach will then go with an offense designed to free his best shooting guards and then position those few rebounders wisely. The Cross Lane Continuity can reach these objectives and many others. Its versatility provides the following outcomes:

1. It creates good shots for two of the three guards.
2. It provides one-on-one opportunities for the best forward.
3. It stations the best inside rebounder on the weak side and swings him to the ball as the offense develops.
4. It guarantees solid defensive balance and consistent offensive board coverage.
5. It functions best against the zone and superstar defenses such as the box and one or triangle and two.

CROSS LANE PERSONNEL

The Cross Lane Continuity is a very simple offense that can be used effectively with a young or inexperienced squad. Each position is a specialized one requiring each player to learn just one role in order to earn good shots.

The players needed to fill the Cross Lane's positions (as shown in Diagram 4-1) are as follows:

Cross Guard (1). He should be an adept passer into the post, a decent shooter, and a crashing rebounder. He must also be capable of defending the break as he is the second guard back.

Key Guard (2). This player should be able to shoot from the free throw circle area and be capable of swinging the ball quickly to the weak side. He must be one of the strongest defenders against the fast break as he is the first guard back.

Strong Post (3). This player is the best inside scoring threat capable of flashing from the weak side and effectively posting up just above the block. He should be adept at tips and weakside rebounding as well as good sealing moves (as discussed in Chapter 3).

Quick Post (4). This is the second best inside scorer and weakside rebounder. An added attribute would be his quickness and one-on-one ability to drive from the short wing area.

Swing Guard (5). This is the best all-around player who can shoot the 15-footer from the corner and pass inside to post players. He is also the team's best shooter most likely to be defended on an individual man basis from the superstar defenses. Player 5 is also expected to hit the boards and is usually the third best rebounder.

The Cross Lane Continuity is best taught initially with each player in a set position, but as it becomes mastered, the players can be gradually interchanged to promote both its versatility and increased team understanding of its concepts.

THE CROSS LANE CONTINUITY'S DEVELOPMENT

Basketball in our area is dominated by the great Boston Celtics' dynasty along with a host of college level teams. Much can be learned from studying such styles of play and by combining their best features into what already is successful in our offensive plans.

The Celtics for years have sent the ball to the baseline to the good shooter who has come from the weak side. His route along the baseline brings his defender into several single or double screens. This is usually done as either a set play or at the end of their fast break.

Boston College's Tom Davis has run a zone offense that is unique in that the attack is specialized by position. Its movements are also based on very sound zone attack principles.

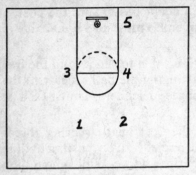

DIAGRAM 4-1
Initial Set

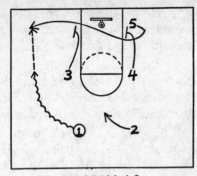

DIAGRAM 4-2
Initial Moves

The Cross Lane Continuity evolved by combining the Celtics' baseline cuts with Boston College's zone attack and merging both styles with our existing Penetration 2-2-1 alignment.

THE CROSS LANE'S CONTINUITY

As diagramed earlier, the Cross Lane Continuity begins with the normal 2-2-1 set. Each time down the floor we go with this set in order to possibly disguise our scoring intentions. The first move is designed to bring our best shooting guard (or forward) 5 to the ball along the baseline route. This move is shown in Diagram 4-2, as cross guard 1 dribbles toward the corner away from swing guard 5. Player 1's dribble signals both strong post 3 and quick post 4 to drop down the lane lines. As 3 is rolling on the ball side, he stops just above the block at the low-post position while continually looking for the ball from 1. Player 1 stops his dribble at the free throw line extended and within his shooting range.

Quick post 4 stops at the weakside low-post position and faces the ball.

Swing guard 5 now begins his baseline move by first backing away from the lane toward the nearest sideline to allow space for post 4 down near the low block area. This minor clear-out allows 5 to determine if he's being played individually on a man-to-man basis as in a superstar defense.

Swing guard 5 now runs his baseline cut, using posts 3 and 4 as stationary screens. He can go either above or below the two screens set by 3 and 4, but he must get to the ballside baseline spot in his shooting range as soon as possible.

Posts 3 and 4 face the ball with a broad stance so they won't be tempted to set illegal screens for 5 as he executes his ballside cut. If 5 is being played on a man basis he should be able to either rub his man off (or at least delay him) on one or both of the screens.

If there is a box and one or a triangle and two being employed, the opposite ballside corner (with but one defender available) is quite vulnerable once swing guard 5 arrives.

Swing guard 5's completed cut places him on the baseline in a straight line with strong post 3 and quick post 4.

Guard 2 now rotates to the top of the key to serve several roles. He must place himself in that area so he can split the seam, using the dribble, between the two nearest defenders. The *splitting of seams* is covered in detail in Chapter 5. This route allows him a good shot if there is any defensive indecision between the two top zone players. Guard 2 is also the fulcrum point that we use to swing the ball to the weak side.

Additionally, 2 can help penetrate the defense by glancing inside to see if either post player is open during the weakside swing. If open, 2 can feed them from the top of the key area.

Finally, key guard 2 must defend the opponents' break should one develop from either a turnover or defensive rebound.

Diagram 4-2 shows the Cross Lane's initial movement as it flattens out the defense and tends to force it into a temporary 2-3 zone-like structure.

Swing guard 5's cut, if timed properly, should get him there as the ball does and certainly before any defender coming out from the lane. Swing guard 5 has now received 1's pass and looks immediately for his baseline jumper.

If 5 is being denied the pass, 1 must look inside quickly to post 3, as two defenders would have each had to make perfect slides to defend both 3 and 5 at the same time. Player 3 could very well be open if 5 is covered and vice versa.

If 5 is defended well after he receives 1's pass and is unable to get off a good shot, he has several options. He must first look inside to 3 down low, who is using strong sealing techniques against the defender assigned to him. Player 5 can best pass to strong post 3 by using a *step-out* pass. This is done by reaching to either side of his defender and passing around him with one hand. This is a pass often used to get the ball out of a double-team. It can be very effective when practiced.

If 3 is being fronted strongly, 5 must improve his passing angle to the post. He does this by either dribbling a bit toward cross guard 1 or passing directly to 1. Player 1 then looks inside to post 3, who now has a much improved chance of receiving a pass. These passing possibilities to post 3 are shown in Diagram 4-3.

If the ball can't be passed into post 3 by 1, it may be because 5's defender is dropping off him and jamming the passing lane. This may open 5 for a return pass and good shot.

If this 1-3-5 triangle creates no inside shots and if 1 doesn't have a decent shot, the ball gets reversed away from 5 as shown in Diagram 4-4. Key guard 2 gets the swing pass and looks for 3, who by now may have effectively sealed his man and will be able to flash up the lane for a quick pass and a strong scoring move.

If neither one of these options develops, quick post 4 pops out high to the free throw line extended and even with guard 1 on the other side.

Guard 2 has several choices here. He can first look inside for strong post 3, who may flash quickly toward the ball. If he is being fronted, the ball can be reversed to 1. Player 1 will then have a good feeding angle to 3. If he was being fronted earlier when the triangle was intact, that indicates he'll be free during his short flash toward 2 with the ball.

Another choice would be for 2 to penetrate the seam existing between the two nearest defenders and pass either right or left when picked up. Or, if no defender is near, he should be open for his free throw area shot.

If none of the above is done, 2 swings the ball to quick post 4 for a possible shot after his pop-out move. As 4 may be closely guarded, his driving opportunities have been increased on the cleared-out side (especially toward the baseline). Player 4 may also have a backcut opportunity if he is being strongly denied the ball. Diagram 4-4 shows all of the various options described above.

After 4 has received 2's swing pass, 5 makes another ballside cut across the lane using 3 as a backscreen and finishes again in his shooting range facing the basket. Player 4 passes to 5 on the baseline and immediately sets up his defender by making a V-cut away from the ball and makes a face cut looking for the give-and-go pass.

This move is particularly effective if 4 is being played closely by a zone defender or on a man basis. This cut is completed in the low-post area just above the block. Player 4 works briefly trying to seal the nearest defender responsible for him.

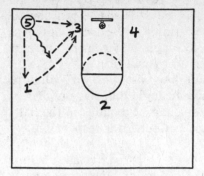

DIAGRAM 4-3
Post Passing

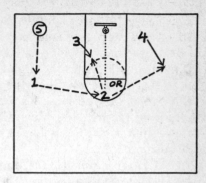

DIAGRAM 4-4
Swing Options

Once 4 begins his give-and-go cut to the low block, guard 1 crosses the lane and replaces 4 on the ballside wing. As 4's defender may have sagged to the lane (or further) to defend 4's give-and-go move, he may not be able to recover in time to defend 1 after 5 passes to him. It is critical that 1 "cheats" slightly toward the basket while replacing 4. This will earn 1 a closer shot as 4's defender is trying to split his coverage between 4 low and 1 at the short-wing position. Diagram 4-5 shows this move.

Once 4 realizes he can't get the ball, he leaves that spot and exchanges with post 3 on the weak side. Player 4 can go to 3's spot by either sliding *up* the lane one step and crossing the lane, or sliding *down* the lane and then crossing over.

POST REPLACEMENT RULE

It is vital that post 3, on the weak side, observes in which direction 4 vacates the low post because his replacement route must be opposite 4's exit route. The *Post Replacement Rule* states that: "When the ballside low post vacates either high or low, the weakside post that enters that same spot must fill it from the opposite direction." If 4 leaves by going up the lane and then across, 3 must fill 4's spot by coming on the baseline side. Conversely, if 4 exits low on the baseline side of the block, 3 must first flash up the lane toward the ball and then slide low to the block.

The obvious reason for these two cuts to be opposite involves 4's original post defender. He will go slightly in the direction of 4's route thinking 4 is trying to improve his posting position. Once 4 really does leave the area, his defender is in poor defensive position to effectively stop a second post player filling in from the opposite direction. Diagram 4-6A shows the low-high replacement cut and Diagram 4-6B shows the high-low replacement.

Post 3 has now filled the ballside low post spot. This fills the third corner of the same 1-3-5 offensive triangle that was previously set up on the left side. Meanwhile, key guard 2 remains in the half-circle area as the Cross Lane's swing position and is responsible for defensive balance.

All four players (1, 3, 4, and 5) have now crossed the lane and are in the same spots as before. The same passing, shooting, and cutting options are not only still present but are open to the same five players who are in their same familiar areas of operation. This breeds great confidence in all players … especially young or inexperienced ones.

Once all options are exhausted on the right side, the ball gets reversed again to 4 on the weak side and the various crossing cuts are executed as shown in Diagrams 4-7A and 4-7B. This action can swing from side to side indefinitely looking for a good shot.

THE CROSS LANE'S
OFFENSIVE REBOUNDING COVERAGE

In order for any offense to be productive, it must have an orderly plan of attack for the offensive boards. Any offense that leaves second shots to chance is one doomed for failure (unless that team has superior talent!).

Our players have individual pre-determined areas that they are

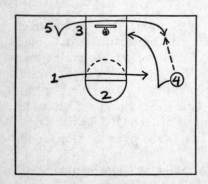

DIAGRAM 4-5
Give and Go

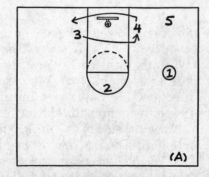

DIAGRAM 4-6A
Low-High Post Cuts

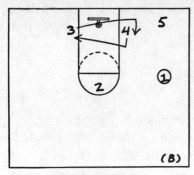

DIAGRAM 4-6B
High-Low Post Cuts

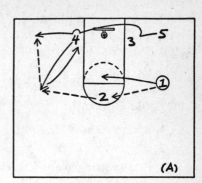

DIAGRAM 4-7A
Cross Lane Swing Set

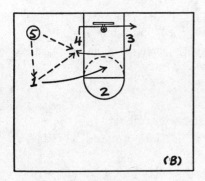

DIAGRAM 4-7B
Post Passing

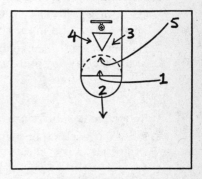

DIAGRAM 4-8
Offensive Rebounding

assigned to on every shot attempt. There is no confusion this way.

Diagram 4-8 shows each player's rebounding coverage. Strong post 3 and quick post 4 must each get to the nearest low block area when any shot is taken. No other player is assigned there, so if one sees that the area is already covered, he simply heads for the other. It is critical that each fights for the inside position between the defender and the board. They are not to watch the ball in flight.

Swing guard 5 must always hustle to the dotted line on the restraining jump circle to form the top point of the rebounding triangle with 3 and 4.

Cross guard 1 is responsible for the area at the middle of the free throw line. His main role is to get to long rebounds or to delay the opponents' outlet pass, which starts their fast break. Player 1's role is half defensive and half offensive in nature.

The remaining player, 2, the key guard, is already positioned at the top of the key. He is allowed to chase only *sure* long rebounds but is never allowed to deny outlet passes to the wing areas.

CROSS LANE POSITIONAL GUIDELINES

Cross Guard (1):

1. Start the Cross Lane Continuity by dribbling to the left wing.
2. Pass to strong post 3 (if open) as he rolls low during your dribble.
3. Pass to swing guard 5 when he has completed his baseline cut.
4. Work your passing triangle enabling you either to shoot or to pass to post 3.
5. If nothing develops, swing the ball to key guard 2.
6. Once quick post 4 begins his give-and-go cut on the opposite side, you must replace him in the shortened "cheat" position.
7. On any shot, fill the free throw shooting spot for offensive rebounds or try to delay any anticipated outlet passes.

Key Guard (2):

1. Rotate the top of circle area as 1 starts his dribble.
2. When you receive your swing pass from 2, look inside quickly to see if strong post 3 is open.
3. Try to catch the swing pass in good shooting position and within your range so you're able to shoot if open.
4. If not open, swing to quick post 4 who is popping out to the short wing. Watch for defensive denial and 4's possible backcut.
5. Remember, you are responsible for defending the opponent's fast break. This implies you can chase a long offensive rebound only when you have a sure chance of getting it. Don't attempt to intercept outlet passes to either wing area.

Strong Post (3):

1. As 1 dribbles to your side, you must roll down the lane to the block looking for 1's pass.
2. Once you are posted and are beginning to seal the nearest defender, you are also being used as a backscreen by swing guard 5. Don't try to help him hang up his defender on your screen ... that is 5's job.
3. Look for passes from either cross guard 1 or swing guard 5 within your 1-3-5 offensive triangle.

4. When the ball gets reversed to 2, try a short flash toward the ball if you were previously being fronted. The defender should now be on your back. If no pass from 2, return to your weakside low-post spot.

5. Remain a weakside rebounder until quick post 4 vacates the ballside low post. Follow the Post Replacement Rule of filling the post from the opposite direction in which post 4 exited.

6. Post up strong, using good sealing techniques against the nearest defender.

7. Crash all offensive boards and fill the nearest low corner of the rebounding triangle.

Quick Post (4):

1. As the cross guard (1) dribbles to the wing to start the offense, you must roll down the lane line to the weakside low post and face the ball. You'll be used as a backscreen for 5, but don't help him ... he's on his own.

2. When the ball is reversed, you must pop out to the short wing area looking for 2's swing pass. Be ready for some defensive denial and a backcut opportunity.

3. Once you've received 2's pass, look to shoot or drive past your defender (the baseline side will be momentarily cleared out).

4. If you have no scoring opportunity, wait for 5's ballside cut along the baseline and give him the ball in his range after he has squared up to the basket in shooting position.

5. After the pass to 5 on the baseline, run a give-and-go move using a face cut. The face cut involves making a V-cut away from the ball first to set up your defender. Then quickly cut between him and the ball. Expect the pass if you are open.

6. If no pass, post low on the ball side just above the block and seal your defender while trying to earn the post pass from either of the two players in your 1-3-5 triangle.

7. Once you realize no post pass is possible you must vacate this position. Your two choices are: (1) slide *up* the lane a step and change with 3 on the weak side; or (2) slide *down* the lane first before exchanging with 3.

8. Your offensive rebounding position is always the nearest vacant low block of the rebounding triangle.

Swing Guard (5):

1. When 1 dribbles to the wing to start the Continuity, you must back up several steps toward the nearest sideline to provide space for 4's roll

move to the low post. When isolated on this side, examine the nearest defender to judge if you are being played with an individual man coverage.

2. Once cross guard 1 has stopped, you must begin your ballside cut to the baseline. You are to use posts 3 and 4 as stationary screens if you are being defended individually. Whether you go above or below the screens is up to you each time you cross to the ball side. Experimentation has shown, however, that it is best if your second screen is used on the baseline side. This permits a quicker "square-up" position in facing the basket. This occurs, of course, only during your first cut as the quick forward 4 is on the wing on each subsequent cut.

3. After catching the ball, look to either shoot or pass to post 3. Your triangle of you, post 3, and cross guard 1 should create a good shot for one of you within a short time span.

4. If no post pass or shot is available, prepare to make another ballside cut along the baseline using 3 as a screen.

5. During any shot you are always to fill the dotted line at the top of the rebounding triangle in the center of the lane.

COACHING GUIDELINES FOR THE CROSS LANE CONTINUITY

1. The Cross Lane's strongest feature is its multiple uses. It is primarily a zone offense but it is equally as valuable against the numerous superstar defenses.

When faced with a box and one defense, we place the individually defended player in the 5 spot.

When faced with a triangle and two defense, we place the two individually defended players in the 4 and 5 spots.

This Continuity also works very well as a delay offense as your delaying tactics can remain "hidden" for a long time. This is especially true if you have already used the Cross Lane as a standard zone offense earlier during the course of the game. Valuable minutes can also be "stolen" quietly by the coach setting a minimum number of swing passes. An example would be that no shot can be taken until a total of five swing passes are thrown.

The multiple uses of the Cross Lane Continuity are a real timesaver for the coach because when he is practicing one offense he is really working on three or four at the same time. His zone, superstar, and delay offenses are all the same when using the Cross Lane Continuity.

2. Develop 5's ability to feed the post effectively by using the step-out pass, as described earlier.

3. During practices and games insist that all five players get to their respective rebounding areas. The triangle's corners, the free throw spot, and the top of the key must all be covered on each shot.

4. Devise pregame warm-up and shooting drills that will practice parts of the Cross Lane Continuity to make its movements automatic.

3-on-1 Triangle Drill (Diagram 4-9)

WHY:
1. To develop 1 and 5's shooting and passing skills.
2. To practice offensive rebounding.
3. To develop quick and purposeful movement in traffic.

HOW:
1. Set up the 1-3-5 triangle on both sides of the lane with one defender (X) in the middle of each triangle.
2. On the right side, 1 passes to 5 for his baseline jumper as X hustles to defend from the middle of the triangle.
3. After 5's shot, 1, 3, and 5 go to their offensive rebounding areas to get a second shot if 5 misses. X also goes to the boards to contest this second shot. X then goes to the right side to await the next triangle.
4. As soon as this 1-3-5 triangle chases its shot, the players exit off the court under the basket and prepare to fill in on the left triangle.
5. The 1-3-5 left triangle does the same, and after their shot, they go to the right triangle.
6. The new 1-3-5 triangle steps on the court on the offensive left and repeats the procedure.
7. Give 5, then 3, and then 1 a total of five shots each from both the left and right sides.

TIPS:
1. Add a second defender so the 3-on-2 triangle becomes more competitive. Let each player shoot when open.
2. Encourage 1 and 5 to use the dribble to improve their respective passing angles.

Swing Shot Drill (Diagram 4-10)

WHY:
1. To give 2 practice in selecting proper scoring options.
2. To develop 4's pop-out and backcut moves.
3. To provide defensive break work for key guard 2.

HOW:
1. Place cross guard 1 with the ball on the right side. Key guard 2 is positioned near the top of the circle. Quick forward 4 is on the weakside post.

2. Place two defenders (X2 and X3) on each elbow and begin X1 at the dotted line on the circle. X2 and X3 can double on 2, back off to play 4 and 1, or play any other form of defense they choose. X1 has the freedom to deny 4 during his pop-out move, pick up 2 with the ball, or "float" in the lane.

3. Player 1 passes to 2, who selects the best options to score. If X2 and X3 double on 2, he can pass off to 1 or 4—whichever is open. If X1 comes up high to play 2, he can pass to 4 as he pops out. If X2 and X3 each back off from 2, he is to split that seam with the dribble until someone either picks him up and he passes off or he can shoot the ball in the 15-foot lane area.

4. After a shot is taken, 4 and 1 go to their respective rebounding areas to rebound against X1 only. X2 and X3 are allowed to chase the long rebounds. On any defensive rebound or turnover, X2 and X3 can fast-break to the far basket against 2 as the lone defender.

5. New players step on the court to begin the drill again.

TIPS:

1. Allow X1 to join X2 and X3 in their fast break against 2. When X1 joins the break, Cross Guard 1 is also on defense to help teammate 2.

2. Match up X1, X2, and X3 so they can switch off with the players in the 1, 2, and 4 spots. Have them run the same drill from the offensive positions except on the other basket.

3. Organize competition between four teams of three players. Whoever scores three baskets first wins the drill and gets excused from the next sprint drill.

Post and Outlet Drill (Diagram 4-11)

WHY:

1. To give 3 and 4 posting and replacement practice.
2. To give 5 work on passing into the post.
3. To practice offensive rebounding.
4. To develop defensive rebounding and outlet passing.

HOW:

1. Place a 5 player in each corner. Place four 1 players on each free throw line extended with two being active at one time. Place two posts (P) above each block on the lane and a third post out-of-bounds nearby waiting to sub in.

2. Place two post defenders in the lane. One is to guard the ballside low post and the other is allowed to "float" in the lane. Place a third defender (X) on 5 who has the ball in the corner.

3. Player 5, with the ball, tries to feed post P as both X defenders play 5 and P. If the ballside post player can't get

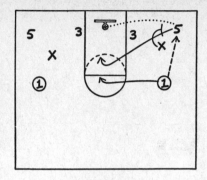

DIAGRAM 4-9

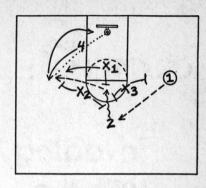

DIAGRAM 4-10

the ball, he empties the post area with either high or low as the weakside post player enters from the opposite direction, as stated in the Post Replacement Rule.

4. When either post gets the ball, he can shoot. On any shot, both posts and 5 go to their offensive rebounding triangle corners. Ballside 1 also goes to the middle of the free throw line.

5. When any defensive X rebounds, he then outlets to the guard 1 on the same side as the defensive rebound. After 1 receives the outlet pass, he then passes the ball to 5 in the corner to continue the drill.

6. The third post rotates in on every fourth play. The three X defenders switch off with the two posts and with 5 on the baseline. After every four plays, exchange a 1 player with a 5 player. All players can then learn each other's positions for better team understanding.

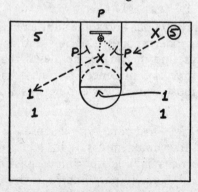

DIAGRAM 4-11

CHAPTER 5:

Invading Zones with the 2-2-1 Gap Attack

The zones are back. Today's motion offenses and great individual players have forced many traditional man teams to adapt the zone as a secondary (and sometimes primary) defense. Pure zones and their perimeter-matching combination defenses have created the need for efficient zone offenses. If the zones are really back, all coaches had better prepare for them.

ZONE PURPOSES

There are many obvious and some subtle reasons for the increasing popularity of modern zones. Coaches and players alike should have a solid background in zone principles if they expect to attack them with any degree of confidence. You must know your enemy to defeat him. The most critical zone purposes are outlined briefly below.

1. Quickly taught. Most zone-type defenses, with their standard slides, are easily diagramed and taught much quicker than man defenses. Most practices include a perimeter passing shell of seven or eight players who alternately pass and hold the ball while the five zoning players perform their slides under the coach's scrutiny. It isn't the most sound teaching method, yet the zone often holds up well considering the minimal practice time.

2. *Lack of mobility/agility.* Teams with good general size may lack the mobility or agility to play strong man defense against superior offensive players. The coach, after judging his available talent, may resort to zones if his material so indicates.

3. *Creates panic.* Coaches often have a temporary fear when seeing the zone in games and unconsciously transmit this same fear to their players. The offensive guard's announcement of "Zone! Zone!" makes everyone pull up cautiously.

4. *Thrives on a lack of offensive patience.* Many players learn the game from the playgrounds. This upbringing often develops the urge to go one-on-one when things get tough. Some players in end-game situations try to take control by themselves, but often end up using solo skills against five well-positioned zone players.

5. *Consumes time late in the game.* Zones are also often used as a change-up defense by teams ahead in the score. A desire to catch up too quickly will force poor shots and minimal offensive rebounding. The zone also seems to get tougher as the lead increases.

6. *Reduces fouls.* Zones are often passive and less apt to foul. Many teams are satisfied to take the outside shot, so the zones defending them seldom need to exert much pressure to stop cutters or drivers. This reduces the chances of bonus free throws occurring too early in each game. Zones also can hide weak or foul-plagued defenders.

7. *Provides some natural traps.* Many zone defenders double-team the ball. Some do it by design; others may do it by accident. Most schoolyard players can cope with one hand in the face but any added defensive hands affect concentration. More passes are also stolen as zoning players can gamble freely knowing their four teammates will protect them from any backdoor cutters.

8. *Triggers the fast break.* Zone defenders are well deployed for strong board control, which starts their breaking game. They may not box out well, but just being closer to the boards provides a good share of rebounds. All five zone defenders are consistently positioned to fill the proper break lanes quickly.

9. *Stymies a great man offense.* The effective man passing games, one-on-one confrontations, and solid screening attacks are all delayed by the zone. Its gang tactics also discourage inside play. This principle is evident during grade school basketball when all nine

players without the ball chase the player with the ball. When the ball gets in the lane it is so easily molested that driving to score is almost impossible. Today's minimal passing skills handicap those trying to get the ball quickly back out against the zone's collapse.

The pros also show each winter that the zone is a desirable defense as they often risk technical fouls trying to execute their camouflaged zones.

10. Develops team unity. A strong helping zone develops the "we" in its team members. Dependence evolves through an awareness of each other's roles.

The *2-2-1 Gap Attack* was built from these principles and has developed through careful analysis and ongoing experimentation. Its simple approach proves that great outside shooting is not necessarily needed to defeat the zone. It is quite versatile in that it attacks any standard half-court zone defense ... whether it's an odd or even front.

There are six zone offense stratagems that lay the groundwork for the 2-2-1's Gap Attack:

1. Dominate the Baseline
2. Attack the Zone's Natural Seams and Gaps
3. Triangulate Players and Passing Lanes
4. "Bully" Selected Defenders
5. Crash Offensive Boards
6. Show Patient Shot Selection

These theories must be totally understood by all of your players so that all phrases are clear. (This information can be used in the Basketball IQ Test, which is discussed in Chapter Three.)

THE GAP ATTACK'S
ZONE-BREAKING PRINCIPLES

1. Dominate the baseline. The Gap Attack works the baseline in a number of ways. Some players begin the offense on the baseline while others cut to that area. One player can successfully freeze two baseline defenders when he changes quickly from one low post to the other.

The ball, itself, is also sent to the baseline area. This forces the zone into long slides, which flatten its shape. This flattening process makes all zones react similarly regardless of their odd or even front. A ball in the baseline area is usually covered by only one player. An added second defender for trapping purposes frees too many passing lanes.

2. *Attack the zone's natural seams and gaps.* This is the Gap Attack's primary thrust. It will be covered in detail later in this chapter.

3. *Triangulate players and passing lanes.* The Gap Attack ruins zones by getting players positioned in triangles so that they can pass quickly in two chosen directions. The triangles provide good release and reverse passes.

4. *"Bully" selected defenders.* The Gap Attack can pinpoint a zone's weak areas very accurately because of its dribble penetration. Each zone has obvious player weaknesses that may vary as the game progresses. A team can zero in their attack toward a great defensive rebounder to draw him away from the boards. Second, an objective may be the bullying of a lazy or weak defender, or one who is in potential foul trouble. Finally, a team may direct their offense away from a quick defender to avoid costly turnovers.

5. *Crash offensive boards.* There are no individual box-out assignments in zone defenses; areas are the main responsibilities when a shot is taken. It then becomes relatively easy for rebounders to knife through defenders to fight for inside positions. The shooter's teammates can anticipate when the shot will be released and can get to the glass providing they don't stare at the ball in flight.

Maintaining offensive board control is also helpful in controlling a strong fast-breaking team. Many teams send only one or two offensive rebounders to the boards and concede the defensive rebounds while trying to delay the outlet pass. The remaining players are sent upcourt to prevent the long threat. The 2-2-1 takes a different approach; it always has 3½ rebounders in the lane hustling for all second shots.

6. *Show patient shot selection.* Our players are taught that zone defenders will *react* to shots where man defenders are instructed to force, or dictate, shots. This "invitation to shoot" gives a shooter confidence that the good shot is always available.

It must also be understood that zone defenses all vary in the time they are able to sustain strong defensive pressure. For example, some teams are very aggressive for the first six passes but they let up after that. Other well-coached teams may maintain this toughness for 12 to 15 passes before dropping back slightly and allowing closer shots. It is the offensive coach's job to determine through scouting how long the opponent's zone will defend with intensity.

A second measurement of this intensity can be judged by the number of weakside swings a team will actively contest. If you reverse the ball three or four times, some zones will fold.

There is also a direct relationship between the amount of time a team stays on defense and the degree of toughness it can sustain. The longer a team remains on defense, the weaker that defense becomes. It is the coach's job to convey to his team the opponents' defensive tendencies. By knowing this, a team can set a minimum number of passes or weakside swings before any shots are attempted.

The 2-2-1 Gap Attack is eaily learned if the terms *seam* and *gap* are understood. A complete explanation of each term is given below.

All zones contain imaginary spaces between any two defenders. We have identified these spaces according to whether a player has the ball or is moving without the ball. If a player has the ball, we are talking of seams. If he doesn't have the ball, we are speaking of gaps.

Seams

A zone's seams are known as *dribbling routes* between any two defenders. When the ball is dribbled along these lines it should exactly split the two nearest players and create indecision on their part concerning which of them is responsible for the advancing dribbler. We call this "taking two" and use it as a game directive when facing zones. This momentary indecision may cause both defenders to stop the ball. This act leaves open both passing lanes behind them that are filled by two 2-2-1 attackers.

Diagram 5-1 shows two basic zone defenses and their respective dribbling seams. Each zone is shown to be "straightened up" or in its beginning alignment. These same seams exist after the zone slides but are at different angles.

Gaps

A zone's gaps are available spaces off the ball between the nearest two defenders. Our 2-2-1 players are taught to step into those gaps when away from the ball. A zone defender's normal focus is on the ball. He can't see the weakside offensive players behind him. The gap player splits the two nearest defenders and faces the ball. Such positioning gives the ball handler good vision of the gap player and creates an open passing lane that was nonexistent before.

Some zone gaps are shown in Diagrams 5-2A and 5-2B. Admittedly, the gaps are ever-changing, but a team's understanding of the concept facilitates the 2-2-1's efficiency against all zones.

The ball is shown attacking each zone's identical seam for ease of explanation. Some remaining weakside offensive players are shown stepping into the existing gaps.

The 1-3-1 zone shows 1 dribbling the seam between X5 and the dropping defender X4. As 1 is "taking two," 2 steps into the X1-X4 gap. Player 3 steps in the gap between X2 and X1. Player 4 is available for a quick flash between X5 and X2.

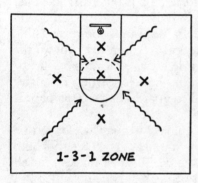

DIAGRAM 5-1A
1-3-1 Zone

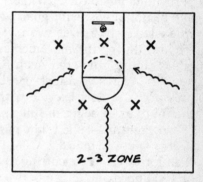

DIAGRAM 5-1B
2-3 Zone

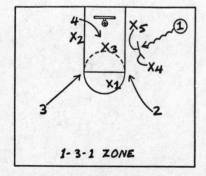

DIAGRAM 5-2A
1-3-1 Zone

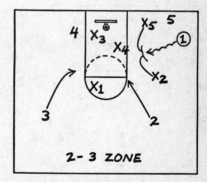

DIAGRAM 5-2B
2-3 Zone

The 2-3 zone is attacked by 1, again dribbling the X5-X2 seam, 2 in the X1-X2 gap, and 3 in the X3-X1 gap.

THE 2-2-1 GAP ATTACK VS. ALL ZONES

Our 2-2-1's alignment and movement against zones are much like our Pass and Pick Continuity that we use to attack man defenses. Diagram 5-3 shows the 2-2-1 set and its player positioning with its triangular passing lanes.

Guards 1 and 2 begin at the lane line extended directly above forwards 3 and 4 at the high elbow post spots. The elbow is located at each junction of the free throw line and the lane lines running perpendicular to the baseline. Center-forward 5 is on either low post and begins opposite the guard with the ball. His mobility from side to side effectively freezes two low defenders. Both must be responsible for him during his movements. His lateral freedom also allows the offense to be "mirrored" as it can start on either side of the court.

The offensive attack can begin several ways. Strong defensive pressure is seldom exerted with guard-to-guard passes. This pass is the first key to begin the offense.

Diagram 5-4 shows the pass from guard 2 to guard 1. Low post 5 begins opposite guard 2. Guard 2, following his pass to 1, splits both high forwards while cutting to the ball side. He then places himself on the approximate gap between the two nearest zone defenders.

Player 1 can then pass directly to guard 2 or he can pass to high forward 3. Forward 3 pivots and relays the pass to guard 2, who is now

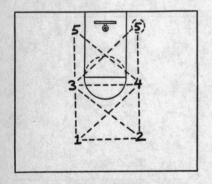

DIAGRAM 5-3

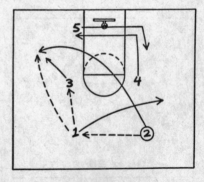

DIAGRAM 5-4

on the seam. After 2's cut, 4 cuts down the lane line on the weak side toward the open ballside low post for an exchange with 5. Player 2 passes to 4 immediately if he is open.

Guard 1 then goes away from the ball placing himself on an imaginary line extending from the basket through the nearest elbow. Player 1's movement away from the ball achieves defensive balance and serves as an ideal position from which to begin reversal of the ball.

Guard 2 has the ball on the seam splitting the baseline and wing defenders. He then starts his penetrating dribble along that seam. His primary objective is to stay on that imaginary line, which splits both defenders in hopes that one or both players will instinctively pick him up. This aggressive seam dribble also "bullies" each of the defenders and forces them to play defense. If neither defender picks him up, he takes the short seam jumper. Should either defender attack him to stop the seam jumper, 2 will pass off quickly to his open teammate. Either 4 on the low post or 3 on the ballside elbow will be open if one of their assigned defenders attacks 2. Diagram 5-5 shows guard 2's seam dribble.

Meanwhile, 5 steps up into the gap on the lane line. This gap exists between the weakside low rebounder and the defender nearest guard 1, as shown in Diagram 5-5. Player 5 places himself in 2's passing vision but stays outside the lane unless his flash to the ball will ensure him the ball and an open shot.

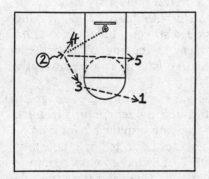

DIAGRAM 5-5
Guard 2 Dribbling
Along Seam

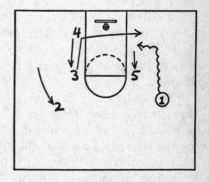

DIAGRAM 5-6
Gap Attack Continues

If 3 gets 2's pass and has no shot, he can swing the ball to 5 or out to guard 1, who then continues the Gap Attack continuity on the other side.

In summary, 2's options during his seam penetration are listed below:

1. Shoot along the seam.
2. Drop off to either 4 down low or to 3 on the elbow.
   a. If 4 gets the pass, he can either shoot or swing the ball to 5.
   b. If 3 gets the pass, he can shoot, reverse the ball to 5, or release the ball to guard 1, who then resumes seam penetration on the other side.
3. Skip pass directly to 5 in the weakside gap for his short jumper.

The offense now continues as shown in Diagram 5-6. As soon as 1 gets the swing pass, 5 slides quickly up the elbow. He must back up the elbow facing the basket so he stays in shooting position should 1 pass to him. This short move up the lane really confuses the weakside defender, as he must also cover 1's attacking seam dribble. Player 3, on the weakside elbow, cuts down the lane line, and then crosses the lane to occupy the new ballside low post. This floods that area with 5 in good shooting range, 3 in the low post spot, and 1 splitting that seam via the dribble. It becomes a 3 on 2 game of keepaway.

Player 4 now steps up into the weakside gap and guard 2 steps up to a point just above the weakside elbow area. Player 1's options, during his seam dribble, are the same that 2 previously had.

This simple rotation continues with both guards attacking the zone's changing seams. The three inside posts continue their rotation in filling the three critical scoring areas in the zone. The ballside elbow, low post, and weakside rebounding gap areas are constantly being occupied.

The three inside players provide great rebounding coverage on the offensive boards. Diagram 5-7 shows how the rebounding triangle is filled by all three forwards with each being responsible for a point on the triangle. Post 3, on the elbow, goes to the dotted line. Low post 4 fills the nearest corner of the triangle. Post 5, in the weakside gap, is in a great area for knifing to the boards and fighting the weakside rebounder for inside position. As he begins from the side post area, he can generate extra momentum while going to the offensive boards. He also has the space and freedom to maneuver over the top or to take the baseline route around the defensive rebounder.

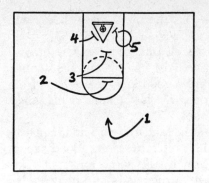

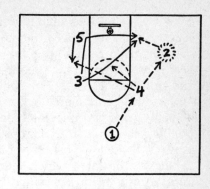

DIAGRAM 5-7   DIAGRAM 5-8

The seam guard also gives another "half" rebounder when he hustles to the free throw spot on the foul line. This position enables him to go either way for a long rebound.

The remaining guard drops back to serve as the defensive "goalie" and stops any long threat.

In game conditions one of my assistant's jobs is to count how many of our players are in the lane on each of our shot attempts. The players then become more cognizant of their responsibilities. We'll sub for players who are "out of the color" consistently.

FREE AGENT ZONE OFFENSE
VS. ALL ZONES

We'll often alter our zone offense slightly for a number of reasons. This is accomplished with our Free Agent Attack. We use it for the following reasons:

1. To capitalize on a superior (or temporarily "hot") shooting guard.
2. To bully specified defenders.
3. As a change-of-pace offense in any given game.
4. To reduce strong defensive post pressure.
5. To serve as a quick-hitting offense when our opponents are ahead and trying to zone us.

The Free Agent Attack stresses that the three inside players run the same basic routes that they run in the 2-2-1 Gap Attack. One guard serves primarily as a feeder and defensive goalie on a permanent basis. The remaining guard is our *Free Agent*. His role is to constantly use free-lance movements off the ball. These moves will eventually bring him to the ball for a good shot.

Diagram 5-8 shows guard 1 passing into post 4. Free Agent 2 begins anywhere in his shooting range. Post 4's first move is to pivot and find Free Agent 2. He should have a good idea where he is from locating his general area before the pass. If 2 is open and in his range, he gets the pass immediately for a shot.

If 4 can't pass to 2, 3 drops down the lane toward 5 and then over to the ballside low post. Player 3's alternate route is to run a diagonal cut down the lane, which places him in the same low spot. This middle cut is always executed in front of the zone's middle defender. Post 4 can pass to 3 on the way through or to guard 2 who can then drop it down to low post 3.

Player 5 runs the normal cut up the lane line on the weak side and finishes either at the side post or on the elbow looking for 4's reversal pass or his own shot.

Post 4 has the following options:

1. Shoot the elbow jumper.

2. Pass to Free Agent 2.

3. Hit post 3 during his diagonal cut to the low post.

4. Hit post 3 during his low lane-crossing flash after his cut toward 5 on the weak side.

5. Swing the ball to weakside 5, who has flashed up the lane line.

Guard 1 always rotates to the weak side for reversal/goalie purposes. The Free Agent now can cut anywhere in his range that he can earn a pass and get off a good shot. Diagram 5-9 shows him cutting across the lane toward 5, who has the ball after 4's swing pass. The three posts' inside rotation continues as 4 runs either the middle cut or down cut to the new low post. Post 3 comes halfway up the lane to step into the gap or to continue up to the elbow.

The Free Agent's movements continue to be unpredictable during the posts' rotation. It must be emphasized to 2 that he always attempts to place himself in the "ball's" vision during his various cuts. Some of the cuts that 2 can use are demonstrated in Diagram 5-10.

After post 4 receives the initial guard pass, he pivots to face the basket and tries to locate 2 in the following situations:

1. Popping out of a single stack down low with center-forward 5

2. Curling around 3 and then toward the ball

3. Stepping into any gap between any two defenders
4. Dropping down to either baseline out of the defenders' vision

The Free Agent Attack's main advantage is the familiar movements that are used once the inside post rotation begins. If this three-man continuity is temporarily slowed down due to strong defensive pressure, the ball is released out to guard 1 and then reentered as soon as possible.

Obviously, 2's chances of receiving the ball are increased when guard 1 can dribble safely on the perimeter while looking for 2.

The rebounding responsibilities are the same as those of the Gap Attack. The Free Agent is the half-rebounder on the free throw line; the three posts fill the triangle; and the back guard is the defensive goalie.

The players claim the Free Agent Attack is fun to play as it has a certain amount of freedom for all. As a coach, I feel this is a positive feature as long as the Free Agent continues to get the ball and take great shots! On the other hand, the defenders feel very confused in practice as they never know where 2 will show up. Young guards like to work on their off-ball movement and shooting skills in hopes that they can someday be the Free Agent.

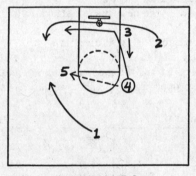

DIAGRAM 5-9

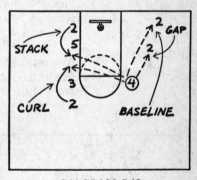

DIAGRAM 5-10

Seam and Second Shot Drill (Diagrams 5-11A and 5-11B)

WHY:
1. To develop guard's seam dribble and shot from both sides.
2. To improve guard's passing abilities.
3. To develop the 3 on 2 keepaway game in a confined area.
4. To develop the offense's 3½ point rebounding triangle.

HOW:
1. Three forwards are placed in low, elbow, and weakside gap areas.

2. Three defenders are in the appropriate post areas and rotate with the offense toward the other side of the floor.
3. Two lines of guards are on each side of the court; each has a ball.
4. The guard on the left side makes a dribble penetration on the seam looking for either a shot or a pass to any one of the three post players.
5. Following any shot, all four offensive rebounders go to their assigned rebounding triangle points to battle the three defenders for the second shots. See Diagram 5-11A.
6. After the shot attempts, the three posts rotate clockwise to the other side of the floor. Player 3 goes to the strongside elbow, 2 to the strongside low post, and 1 to the weakside gap area. The penetrating guard goes to the other guard line on the opposite side of the court after his penetrating seam movement.
7. The guard on the right side then continues the offense from the other side. After the shot, the four offensive rebounders again crash to their assigned spots. See Diagram 5-11B.

TIPS: 1. Watch the guards' eyes to make sure they look up.
2. Have the posts experiment with the return pass to the guard for his shot during the 3 on 2 keepaway.
3. Have posts rotate quickly for the new guard's attack following the previous shot.
4. Have posts replace in counterclockwise direction.
5. Have posts and defenders switch roles.
6. Chart which side of the court has the most scoring success.
7. Insist that the posts use proper pivots and shots as described in Chapter 8.

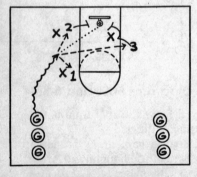

DIAGRAM 5-11A

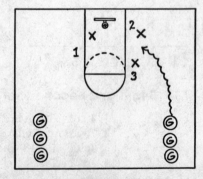

DIAGRAM 5-11B

Shoot and Follow Drill (Diagram 5-12)

WHY: 1. To improve shooting, rebounding, and passing of all players.
       2. To develop offensive quickness.
       3. To polish the team's competitiveness.

HOW: 1. Guards line up on one side of court. Each has a ball.
       2. Two posts line up—one on the strongside elbow (E) spot, and the other in the weakside gap (G) spots.
       3. Guards (S) dribble along the imaginary seam line and take the jump shot within their range.
       4. G and E go to their respective triangle points and then rebound either the missed or made shots.
       5. The first one to the ball rebounds and quickly passes to the other. The receiver takes a quick shot while the passer applies passive defense. The shooter follows his shot, rebounds, and then passes to the player who just passed to him. He, too, plays passive defense on the shot.
       6. Shooter S goes to his half-rebound spot on the foul line. If a long rebound comes to him, he passes inside to either G or E and they each shoot, rebound, and pass to their partner as before. G and E must each get a shot.
       7. After G and E both shoot, a new group of S, G, and E players step out and continue the drill.

TIPS: 1. After the team learns the drill, make it competitive by having each group of three players keep score to see who gets a designated number of points first. A good score to start with would be 30 points. The guards' shot counts 2 points and the posts' inside shots count 1 point each.
       2. Use the left side of the court on alternate days.
       3. Instead of a 30-point game, have a three-minute time limit.

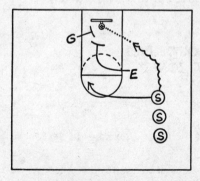

DIAGRAM 5-12

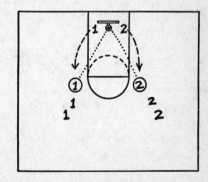

DIAGRAM 5-13

The Brown Game (Diagram 5-13)

WHY: 1. To develop shooting accuracy under pressure.
         2. To build teamwork.

HOW: 1. Two teams of three players each line up at each elbow (or
            other area).
         2. Each front player has a ball and a partner rebounds in front.
         3. Player 1, in front, shoots a total of five shots and alternates
            each shot with the front shooter in the 2 line. Each basket
            counts one point but a shot that drops cleanly through,
            hitting all-net, receives two points.
         4. After each player takes his five shots he goes to rebound for
            the next shooter on his team.
         5. A cumulative score is kept between each team. Both teams
            play a four-quarter game with each shooter responsible for
            his brace of five shots.
         6. The Brown Game is over after the fourth period and the
            respective scores are called.

TIPS: 1. Use both main baskets with six players per basket.
         2. Play a consolation and championship round later in the
            practice or on the following day to enhance anticipation of
            future competition.
         3. The Brown Game was invented by Ron Brown, one of my
            former players who was a great player and is an even greater
            person. I promised to give him credit if I ever used his drill
            in a book. This tip is to appeal to your players to help
            develop coaching techniques. Make them be a part of the
            game's development.
         4. The selected shooting spots in the Brown Game can be on
            any area that your offensive attack tries to get shots from.
         5. Use the scoreboard to keep score. This gives the game a new
            twist.

2-2-1 COACHING GUIDELINES
FOR ATTACKING ZONES

1. Stress beating the zone with the *posts*, not the guards. They are only
   a supplement.
2. All guards must be able to use two-handed ball fakes to best move
   defenders.
3. Our players are convinced that zones are easy to beat because we
   don't use many ourselves. Zones are a sign of possible weakness.

4. An organized passing attack combined with quick player movement will beat zones. No defender can move quicker than the ball.

5. Emphasize that the chest pass is thrown from one chest to another chest. If passes can hit the "numbers," the shooter will be able to deliver the shot quickly.

6. Guards must look inside to read the zone's seams as the zone stretches to match cutting players.

7. A zone is much less of a zone if each defender can be made responsible for a potential scorer.

8. If the 2-2-1 team lacks talented post size, it is advisable to insert smaller players with quickness to capitalize on the many one-on-one situations that develop in this offense.

9. The objective is to force any defender to guard one offensive threat with the ball and at the same time have a second offensive player either cutting to or positioned in the vacated area. The defender must either attack the new threat with the ball or retreat to the original area to stop the player behind him.

CHAPTER 6:

Attacking Man-Zone Defenses with Three 2-2-1 Attacks

Sooner or later, most coaches will have an exceptional scorer. This player may operate from either a guard or a forward position and may occasionally be a center. Whether this player is developed within the system or arrives as a transfer student, you must be prepared for some form of combination or "junk" defense designed to take your best scorer out of the team's normal offensive plans.

WHY THE MAN-ZONE DEFENSES?

Today's standard zones can't handle the exceptional scoring guard or forward. The scoring skills of these players are developed to an extremely high level of play. A passive zone often falls victim to great shooting or penetration by talented guards or forwards. A high scoring center, however, is usually best contained with a conventional zone approach as his operational area is close to the basket.

Many coaches start their one best defender regardless of his marginal offensive skills. This is done in an attempt to maintain an emphasis on team defense. The superior defender is often used to shut down an opponent's leading scorer and often does so from some type of special stacked defense. The denial of passing lanes to the superstar is often intensified by the four players positioned behind him in a zone. The defender knows that any attempted gamble, which fails, will find the player quickly absorbed by the remaining zone players. He can then quickly reattach himself to the assigned star.

Coaches often post the opposing star's scoring average on the team bulletin board so the whole team can be motivated to share the job of keeping the great scorer under his season's average. Shot charts from scouting trips are also posted to indicate the star's shooting range along with his preferred spots on the floor. The chosen man-zone defense will then focus its efforts on forcing the superstar away from these areas.

The superstar defense also permits a coach the luxury of playing taller, less agile players in the zoned structure of the defense. This strong rebounding edge may be the difference in the closing moments of a game when the outcome is not dependent on scoring but on the one big defensive rebound so necessary in preventing the game-winning second shots.

Coaches will also go with a box and one on the point guard who runs the offensive "show," even though the guard, himself, may not be a great scorer. The philosophy behind such a move centers on forcing the shooting guard rather than the point guard to initiate the attack. This tends to throw off the team's offensive rhythm.

TYPES OF SUPERSTAR DEFENSES

Superstar defenses fall into two basic categories, which depend on whether the team must contend with either one or two great scorers.

Teams with only one high scoring guard or forward will see either the box and one or the diamond and one defense. The box and one is often used if the normal offensive set runs two guards whether or not one of the guards is the high scorer. This defense and its slides are shown in Diagram 6-1.

The diamond and one is best utilized when the opponents run an offensive set using a single guard. This structure is also used regardless of whether the great scorer is a guard or forward. The diamond and one with its slides are shown in Diagram 6-2.

The second basic category of superstar defenses is that of the triangle and two. This alignment is used in an attempt to zero in on

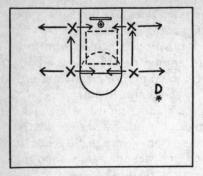

DIAGRAM 6-1

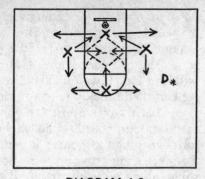

DIAGRAM 6-2

two great scorers regardless of their offensive positions. The triangle and two is also used as an off-beat or "junk" defense in order to confuse the offense. Many coaches use it as a standard defense against the sideline play, for one total possession following a time-out, or even as an opening defense of a big game, simply to surprise and disorganize an opponent.

The triangle and two, if not seen regularly, will confuse the well-coached team, as the players won't know whether to run their man or zone offense against it. This momentary delay in offensive rhythm may find several "zoned" players standing around wondering what to do next while the "manned" players without the ball are trying to shake their defenders free. This lack of offensive action can destroy a team's tempo and result in a few turnovers. It may also produce some unpracticed shots followed by unfamiliar board coverage.

The triangle and two has been played with a number of variations all designed to produce some "stand around" time and reduce the normal teamwork promoted when using a total five-player scoring attack.

One of the triangle and two defenses recently popularized is the position of the bottom three defenders as if in a 2-1-2 traditional zone. The remaining two defenders will match up man-to-man with the opponent's best guard and forward. This is shown in Diagram 6-3.

Another variation is the traditional bottom three in a triangle zone and the top two defenders playing both offensive guards on a man-to-man basis. This is shown in Diagram 6-4.

Another method is the triangle and double. This is designed to stop just one great player during a last-second shot situation where percentages indicate the shot will be taken by the team's best scorer. Here the bottom triangle within the lane is played as before, but the

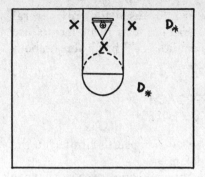

DIAGRAM 6-3

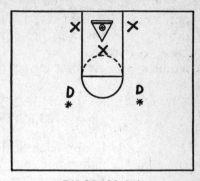

DIAGRAM 6-4

two-man defenders double-team the great shooter before and after the inbound pass. The inbounder is usually ignored. This defense is used sparingly but usually after a time-out for an obvious last shot with limited time remaining. This is shown in Diagram 6-5.

The final illustration showing the triangle and two is the most recent innovation. The man defenders' options remain the same as before but the three-player triangle is inverted, leaving the single player under the basket while the two best rebounders form the base of the triangle below the free throw line. Diagram 6-6 shows the triangle and two with the inverted triangle.

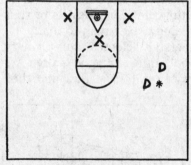

DIAGRAM 6-5

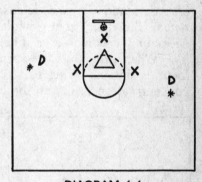

DIAGRAM 6-6

WEAKNESSES OF SUPERSTAR DEFENSES

The superstar defenses are compensatory in nature as they are trying to cover up a weakness. They are structurally unsound, and careful probing into them will present both good shots and offensive board strength. They are also weak in execution, since most teams don't practice them often. They are usually used for only several practice sessions in preparation for a specific team. This lack of use hardly strengthens a team's defensive confidence. The players on both teams know it is a secondary defense at best.

THE 2-2-1's APPROACH TO SUPERSTAR DEFENSES

The 2-2-1's approach to the superstar defenses is limited to the three basic combination, or "junk", defenses.

Because the diamond and one and box and one are so similar, we attack them both in the same way. The only difference exists when the single defender plays our guard or our forward. We run a separate offense when our guard is being denied the ball and yet another if our forward is being played individually.

Even though the triangle and two can be played a number of ways as described earlier, we run just one attack against it. This doesn't vary when the internal triangle is inverted leaving the single player under the basket. It also makes no difference whether our guards or forwards are being played on a man-to-man basis.

Although they are designed for the combination defenses, these offensive continuities can also be used as set plays or regular offenses against standard zone defenses. They are all versatile enough to defeat traditional zones, while exploiting the scoring skills of your special high scorer—even if he is *not* being played man-to-man.

When attacking the various superstar defenses, our primary focus is not on trying to force the ball into our good scorer. We concentrate on directing the ball away from him at first and then

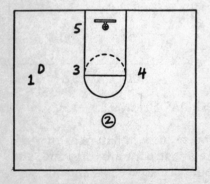

DIAGRAM 6-7   DIAGRAM 6-8

bringing the scorer toward the ball from the weak side. This is done using multiple screens set by the interior lane cutters along with the zone defenders themselves. It is vital that the inside players get ample chances to score while running these offenses. Each player must be made to feel as an integral part of the attack rather than just an ornament while the emphasis is placed on the scorer. These players understand that, if they run their routes properly, they will earn good scoring opportunities.

ATTACKING THE BOX OR DIAMOND AND ONE

Freeing the Guard with the Rub Offense

When facing a box or diamond and one, it is imperative that the three forwards still operate from their normal Penetration positions on the low post and elbow areas. Standard zone attacking principles must be followed, as four-fifths of the defense still remains a zone.

All four corners of the box or diamond are defended by the zone players. Our *Rub* Offense, however, places only three posts in the zone's four corners. This seems, at first, to simplify the defense's responsibilities, thus freeing one defender to help out wherever he can. This thought is quickly eliminated as the three post players are constantly rotating into the four defensive corners. Now each of the four defenders realizes that he is either in the process of protecting his area, or, after one rotation, he will have a post player in his area. This rotation allows the three posts to occupy all four defenders whether they are in the box or diamond structure.

Diagram 6-7 shows the original positions of the Rub Offense prior to any movement. We place superstar guard 1 on the same side of the floor as center-forward 5. He is being denied the ball by defender D. Our two forwards 3 and 4 begin on both elbow positions. Our best passing guard, 2, starts at the top of the key.

Diagram 6-8 illustrates the offense as it is being run toward the right side. As guard 2 dribbles toward the right, this signals the three forwards 3, 4, and 5 to begin their internal rotation within the zone. During all cuts they face the ball with high hand targets. This presents the passing guard 2 with exact visual areas, congests the lane area a bit more, and impedes the defenders' slides.

As forward 3 drops toward the baseline, guard 1 begins a lane cut from the weak side toward the ball. It is critical that when 3 drops toward the baseline he does it while facing the lane and sliding sideways as if playing defense. This sideways stance provides a broad target for guard 1 to Rub his defender D, off 3's moving screen. This inward facing direction also reduces 3's chances of intentionally screening D and getting a foul. He can't know just by facing the lane when 1 and D are coming through. Additionally, this side stance places 3 in a perfect rebounding position should a shot materialize from the strong side.

Post 4 backpeddles from his strongside elbow area to 3's original elbow position. Again, this is done with hands held at head height to slow down the defense's slides and to create a better target for the guard 2. He finishes in a high position that enables him to crash the offensive boards and to occupy the top of the imaginary rebounding triangle at the dotted line of the jump circle.

Center-forward 5 cuts across the lane as guard 2 begins his dribble. C-F 5 then flashes up toward 4's original elbow spot while looking for the ball. This flash up the lane is again executed with a wide hand target for 2's possible pass. C-F 5's cut toward the ball is done after 3 begins his weakside drop toward the baseline. This slight delay allows guard 1 a second obstacle upon which to Rub off defender D during his strongside cut. If 1's defender is not stopped by rolling post 3, he may then be hung up on 5.

As guard 1 catches 2's pass, he looks for his shot or further penetration followed by a closer shot. Guard 2 has no defensive pressure while making the pass to guard 1, so each pass should be perfect with guard 1 receiving the ball at chest height for a quick release.

The low defender on 5's defensive corner tends to move up the lane several steps with him. This momentarily leaves the strongside low area open for a possible quick drive by guard 1 or a pass to 3, who has quickly cut from the weakside low post to the strongside post.

Diagram 6-9 shows the completed cuts after the first rotation of all five players. Guard 1 has the ball with the following options:

1. shoot
2. drive
3. pass to 5 on the strongside elbow
4. pass to 3 who has rotated to the strongside post

If none of these options is available, the ball is released to guard 2, who now swings the offense to the left side of the court.

As the ball is reversed via 2's dribble, the same inside routes are run again by the three posts. When the ball is released to guard 2, post 3 quickly cuts back across the lane to the strongside low post and waits for 5's drop toward the baseline. Post 4 then backpeddles toward the weakside elbow just held by 5.

Meanwhile, 1 begins his cut again through the congested lane in an attempt to shake his defender. This continuity is shown in Diagram 6-10 as guard 2 changes sides of the floor while looking for guard 1 to pop out of the other side.

As guard 1 receives the ball, he has the same options open to him that he had when on the other side.

Diagram 6-11 shows the offense completed on the left side of the floor with the ball at guard 1. Again, if none of the same options develops, the ball is released to passing guard 2 and the offense continues on the offensive right.

This offense creates good shots for the pressured guard along with open passing lanes to his teammates on all four corner spots. Good board coverage is provided along with consistent defensive balance by guard 2. The Rub Offense is an excellent choice as a zone attack for a team fortunate to have a great shooting guard, whether or not he is being played on a man basis individually.

Freeing the Forward with the Pop and Swing Offense

If our great scorer is a forward, we run our Pop and Swing Offense. This pattern starts with the other two forwards, 3 and 4, located low on the blocks. Both guards are called upon to screen the zone and reverse the ball to the weak side. Our forward 1, being played on a man basis by D, starts on the baseline opposite guard 2 on the offensive right as shown in Diagram 6-12. One guard, 5, starts at

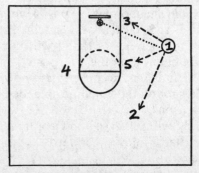

DIAGRAM 6-9

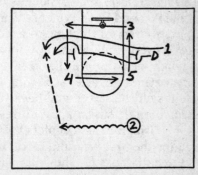

DIAGRAM 6-10

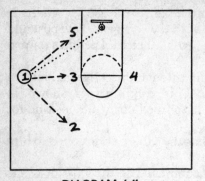

DIAGRAM 6-11

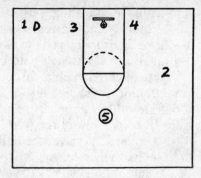

DIAGRAM 6-12

the top of the key and the other guard, 2, begins opposite forward 1. Guard 2 plays the area of a normal wing on the free throw line extended.

As guard 5 dribbles to the right side, forward 1 begins a route from the weak side to the strong side as he attempts to rub his defender D off post 3 and then off strongside post 4. Post 3 faces the lane with elbows at shoulder height and hands up. This presents a wide screen into which forward 1 directs his defender. Post 3, by staying still and facing inward, ensures a legal screen.

As forward 1 is making his way around 3 and then post 4, the guard positioned on the ball side looks to screen the nearest defender at the ballside elbow. His job is to temporarily screen him inward allowing guard 5 to dribble freely and then pass to forward 1 with minimal defensive pressure.

After 5 has passed to 1, his next move is the weak side. Forward 1 now has the ball and has lost his defender during his baseline cut. Diagram 6-13 shows the cuts of each player during the first phase of the Pop and Swing Offense. Forward 1 can shoot or pass to post 4 who has moved up the lane to a side post. Post 3, on the weak side, is in good rebounding position for any shot. When 3 sees that 1 will not shoot, he comes to the strong side just below 4 on the side post.

Guard 2, after screening in the high defensive corner man, now slips off the screen and backs out to a spot on the lane line extended for both defensive and ball reversal reasons.

Diagram 6-14 depicts the Pop and Swing Offense and 1's options after the first rotation, including the guards' moves. Forward 1, with the ball, looks for the following options:

    1. shoot

2. drive to baseline for a jumper

3. pass to 4 on the side post

4. pass to post 3 who has cut across the lane to a point below 4

If none of these develops, the ball is released to guard 2 who dribbles to the left. After 1 releases to 2, he uses 3 and 4 as a temporary double screen for his defender who may have attached back to him. He repeats his cut to the new ball side as the offense continues on the left side. Reversal of the ball is done with no strong defensive pressure as the top defensive players of the box or diamond are not likely to extend their structure to challenge his dribbling. Weakside guard 5 may be open for 2's quick swing pass and an open shot, as shown in Diagram 6-15.

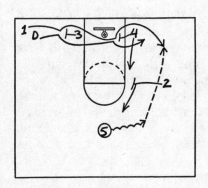

DIAGRAM 6-13

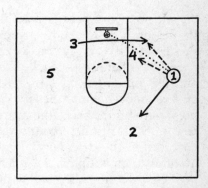

DIAGRAM 6-14

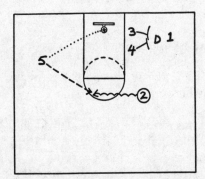

DIAGRAM 6-15

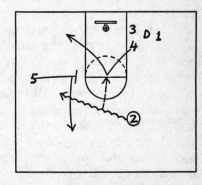

DIAGRAM 6-16
Offense Changes
to Left Side

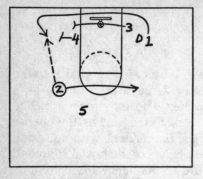

DIAGRAM 6-17
Guard Hits 1

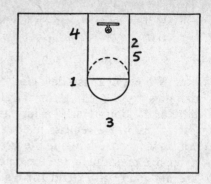

DIAGRAM 6-18
Diagonal Set

If no swing pass is possible to 5, 2 dribbles to the left and 4 flashes up high to the free throw shooting spot looking to split the middle of the defensive box or diamond. Player 2 passes to 4 if he is open. If 4 is being covered, he continues his roll to the new strong side and sets up on the medium post as before. Diagram 6-16 shows the offense's movement to the left. Weakside guard 5, seeing there will be no pass to him, screens the nearest defensive cornerman inward as 2 continues his dribble. Forward 1 then runs his cut through the flexing zone, using the defenders plus the double screen of 3 and 4 in an attempt to hang up his defender, D.

Guard 2 enters the ball to the cutting forward 1, who now has the same options as before. Player 2, after passing to 1, immediately cuts away to the weak side as the screening guard 5 rolls off his screen and backs straight out for purposes of defensive balance and weakside reversal. This is shown in Diagram 6-17.

Post 3 then runs the same cut across the lane to form a double post with 4. It is crucial that the passing guard 2 go weak side immediately after his pass to forward 1. He is the only weakside rebounder and is responsible for board coverage on that side.

This offense continues with an emphasis on getting the ball to forward 1 for a shot or a drive after he has eluded his defender off the double screen set by posts 3 and 4. Additional scoring opportunities are available for both post 4, during his lane cut, and for 3 going from post to post down low. In addition, guards 1 and 2 can score from the quick swing pass.

In summary, this offense emphasizes the scoring of a good forward who is being denied the ball but it is also versatile enough to be used as a regular zone offense designed for a scoring forward. Yet, it still gives great shots for the other players. A coach may choose to run this Pop and Swing Offense as the basic zone attack if his material is suitable. In that case, the coach is already well prepared for the superstar defense should it come his way.

ATTACKING THE TRIANGLE AND TWO DEFENSES

The triangular aspect of this defense is positioned primarily for strong board coverage with minimal straight defensive help on the perimeter. The two man-to-man defenders may play any two offensive players so it is much easier to develop only one offense regardless of whether our guards or our forwards are being overplayed.

The Diagonal Offense is an off-shoot from the regular sideline play. It involves the two superstars directly as screeners for each other. They have enjoyed playing it as it is fun to explore the options available. The two players who have team scoring utmost in their mind can earn a lot of great shots for both each other and their three teammates.

Diagram 6-18 shows the alignment for the Diagonal Offense with the two superstars, 1 and 2, set up opposite each other. Player 1 is at the elbow and 2 is across the lane on the opposite side post. Player 3 is the best passing guard while post 4 is the best rebounder. Player 5 is both a strong screener and mobile rebounder.

Guard 3 starts the offense by dribbling toward 1 at the near elbow. As soon as 3 starts his dribble, 1 cuts across the lane toward his teammate's defender who is playing 2 man-to-man. Player 1 then sets a headhunt screen on 2's defender. The weakside superstar, 2, now has a choice of two cuts. Diagram 6-19 shows 2 cutting high to the elbow that 1 just vacated. Player 1's screen should force a defensive switch that will free both of them as they come toward the ball.

The original screener, 1, after seeing 2's high cut, simply cuts opposite him around low post 4. Guard 3 then passes to either 1 or 2 as they come ball side.

If the weakside 2, after 1's screen, chooses to go low and around post 4, then 1 takes the opposite route and returns up high toward guard 3 with visible hand targets. The ball is again passed to either scorer for an open shot. If the low defender on the triangle comes out to defend 2 who received the pass, then 4 is open for a short pass and an easy shot. This is shown in Diagram 6-20. Player 5 stays on the

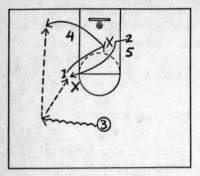

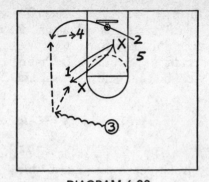

DIAGRAM 6-19   DIAGRAM 6-20

weak side for boards and guard 3 remains behind the ball for defensive balance and ball reversal purposes.

The Diagonal Offense continues by passing the ball back out to 3, who dribbles across the top of the key. The ball reversal is, again, very easy because there are no defenders near the dribbling guard. Weakside rebounder 5 comes high setting a side screen for 1 on the elbow as 3 starts his dribble. After the screen, 1 moves parallel with the ball toward the weakside elbow. Screener 5 then drops to the weakside post as he did on the other side of the floor. Post 4 crosses the lane late, then sets up low as before on the ball side. Player 2, on the weak side, now moves up the lane beside 5 on the side post as before. See Diagram 6-21.

Guard 3 can hit 1 up high. The right side is now cleared out for 1's possible drive or shot. If this is not available, the Diagonal Offense is now reset and ready to be run on the right side. Player 1, on the strong side, crosses the lane setting a screen on the weakside 2's defender and then goes opposite his cut. It is vital that the screener observes whether the cutter goes either high or low. He must go opposite the cutter coming high; the screener, 1, after seeing this high cut, quickly goes low around 4. Guard 3 then passes to either of the open players as rebounder 5 covers the weakside boards. In the event neither player is open, the ball is released back to 3 as 5 comes toward him to set the screen on 2 and run the offense toward the left. This is seen in Diagram 6-22.

The Diagonal Offense creates good shots for both great scorers regardless of their normal playing positions. The options available to them make the offense very unpredictable. Scoring balance is provided as the two superstars will get many shot attempts during the normal offensive flow, as will the two inside players.

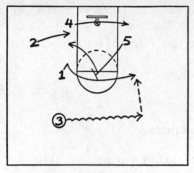

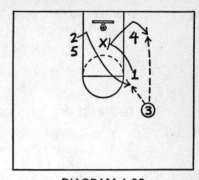

DIAGRAM 6-21   DIAGRAM 6-22

We, as coaches, like to operate within a small margin of error in our constant drive to earn shots before turnovers. The Diagonal Offense reduces such turnovers as the ball is usually in the hands of the two best players.

Its principles are based on sound offensive theories that are used in attacking both straight zone and man defenses. The two-man screening game along with the many stationary and repeated screens of players 1 and 2 will effectively attack the man defenses. Conversely, the low screens, weakside swings, and strong offensive rebounding positions make the Diagonal Offense an excellent attack to beat the standard dropback zones.

The Diagonal Offense can serve very well as an all-purpose offense that will maximize the scoring output of any team's two best shooters.

COACHING TIPS IN TEACHING OFFENSE VS. SUPERSTAR DEFENSES

1. Keep the superstar away from the ball initially and then bring him to it later.

2. Remind your players to have offensive patience.

3. Stress that all offensive players are potential scorers in each of the attacks.

4. Consider using a superstar offense as your basic or auxiliary zone attack, even if faced with standard zone defenses most of the time.

5. Have the superstar practice free throws often, as teams often use more than one defender in a game to guard him. They are usually

encouraged to foul freely knowing that each player can use all his fouls, if necessary, to contain the great scorer.

6. Stress to your team that a superstar defense is an unpracticed defense.

Rub Lead-Up Drill (Diagram 6-23)

WHY:
1. To develop 1's shooting and timing.
2. To improve 2's passing to 1.
3. To teach guard 1 his different cutting routes.
4. To develop 3 and 5's shooting.
5. To encourage team rebounding.

HOW:
1. Start guard 1 on left side with no defense on him.
2. Player 3 is high and 5 is low on same side.
3. Guard 2 begins his dribble to the right as 3 drops and 5 crosses the lane and then flashes up along the lane line to the elbow.
4. Player 1 makes his cut through the lane rubbing shoulders (to ensure a perfect screen) with 3 and/or 5. He then comes out on the ball side and guard 2 passes to him for a shot. Cutter 1 can run the following routes:

   a. Under 3 and under 5
   b. Under 3 and above 5
   c. Above 3 and above 5
   d. Above 3 and under 5

5. Guard 2 can lob a pass to 3 on the baseline for his shot or to 5 flashing up for his power move into the lane.
6. Players 3, 5, and 1 rebound all shots.
7. After the first guard passes to guard 1, the next guard on the left side dribbles to the right side and he, too, passes to 1 for a drive or shot.
8. After 1's drive and shot options, the third guard dribbles from left to right and passes to 1, who immediately returns the ball to 2 for 2's reversal of the offense, including 1's cut from right to left.
9. For reversal of offense, 5 drops and crosses the lane while 3 comes up high as 1 cuts the lane. During any cut, 1 can choose to finish his cut on the baseline or anywhere on that side of the floor within his shooting range.
10. Both remaining guards on the right repeat their dribbles to the left side and pass to guard 1 for his shot, drive, and return pass.

TIPS: 1. Add a defender to guard 1.
            2. Add post 4 at the right elbow.
            3. Gradually add defenders until a box or diamond is completed with four players.
            4. Have four defenders switch between a box and a diamond.
            5. Insist that all shots are rebounded by all offensive players except passing guard 2. Guard 2 must hit anyone open.
            6. Play a "Six" Game: Give six possessions and the offense must score on three of them in order to avoid a sprint drill. This stresses offensive patience.

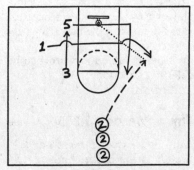

DIAGRAM 6-23

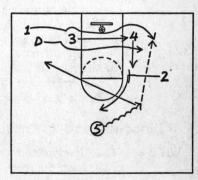

DIAGRAM 6-24

Pop and Swing Lead-Up Drill (Diagram 6-24)

WHY: 1. To develop 1's lane cut and timing.
            2. To develop weakside swing shot for guards.
            3. To create shots for 4's flashing move.
            4. To maintain offensive continuity.

HOW: 1. Set all five players in the Pop and Swing alignment.
            2. Player 5 dribbles away as 1 runs his defender, D, into screens set by 3 and 4.
            3. Player 5 passes to forward 1 for his shot as he goes one-on-one versus D.
            4. Players 5 and 2 perform their Pop and Swing moves.
            5. After shot, 1, 3, and 4 crash boards for a tip-in on a miss, or they retrieve the ball after a made shot and outlet the ball to guard 2 on the offensive right. Player 1 then comes ball side quickly as 3 and 4 set a double screen for 1 on D.
            6. Player 2 then dribbles toward the weak side and can do one of the following:
               a. Hit 4 on his flash to the foul line.

        b. Swing to weakside guard for his shot.

        c. Return ball to 1 for a shot if his defender elects to avoid the screen by "cheating" into the lane.

    7. On any of the above, all but the passing guard must go to their respective rebounding areas.

TIPS: 1. Gradually add defenders until the four player box or diamond structure is completed.

    2. Have the four players determine which defense they'll use for a set number of possessions. Example: go with the box for three times; the diamond for two times; back to the box four times; then go with the diamond for one possession. This makes all offensive players run their routes accurately and the passing guard rewards them with the ball if they are open.

    3. Alternate several of your best defenders on forward 1 so he can experience different defensive reactions.

    4. Play a "Six" Game as described earlier.

Diagonal Lead-Up Drill (Diagrams 6-25A and 6-25B)

WHY: 1. To develop teamwork and timing between players 1 and 2.

    2. To have the receiver square-up to the basket immediately upon catching the ball.

    3. To improve rebounding on all shot attempts.

    4. To explore all shooting opportunities for all players.

HOW: 1. Initially use only passing guard 3 along with the two superstars, 1 and 2, as offensive players, along with the two defenders assigned to 1 and 2.

    2. Place 1, 2, and 3 in the Diagonal set and have 3 begin the drill by dribbling toward 1 at the elbow. See Diagram 6-25A.

    3. Player 1 then screens 2's man on the weak side as 2 comes ball side to either the elbow or the low post.

    4. Player 3 passes to whoever is open; the shot is taken, and both "stars" hustle for inside rebounding positions.

    5. After the shot attempt (whether it is made or missed), 1 and 2 outlet to 3 at the lane line extended and get to their high and low spots as before the shot was taken. Defenders pick up as quickly as possible.

    6. Player 3 continues the Diagonal attack by dribbling toward the offensive right as the top player rolls along the free throw line and parallel to the ball toward the elbow. See Diagram 6-25B.

    7. Once there, the high "star" screens away for low "star" who

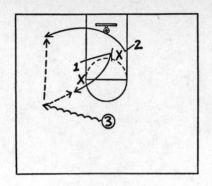 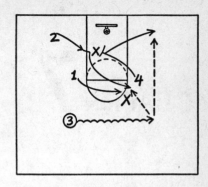

DIAGRAM 6-25A   DIAGRAM 6-25B

again runs either of the two available routes. Both come out on the ball side low post and elbow.

8. Guard 3 again feeds the open "star" for a shot attempt; they rebound, then outlet the ball to resume the offensive motion to the left side as before.

TIPS:

1. Switch defenders on players 1 and 2.

2. Place the defensive triangle in the lane and mix it up by aligning the triangle either straight or inverted as discussed earlier.

3. Add low post 4, who always crosses to the ball side and then receives the drop pass from a "star" if he is open.

4. Add high screener 5 and pass to him if he is open during either his posting or screening moves.

5. Play a "Six" Game as described earlier.

CHAPTER 7 :

Capitalizing on the Penetration's Delay Games

Each year, many games are lost because teams are unable to preserve leads. Pressure defenses operate with nothing to lose when attacking teams that are hesitant to shoot. Any form of delay attack must attempt to score.

Delay games have also become especially popular with teams that are scheduled to play a highly touted opponent with no apparent chance to win. They feel a slowdown will shorten the game and increase chances of winning or at least keep a respectable losing margin.

There is no place for such a mental approach in coaching. There may be a slightly improved chance to win but the overall result is a poor one. Fans will not consistently support the slowdown style. It's just not an exciting brand of ball that will recruit or motivate players at any level.

There is, however, a need for limited strategic usage of the delay game which is within the realm of exciting, competitive basketball. These delay purposes will be discussed below.

WHY DELAY?

1. *To destroy the opponent's offensive and defensive continuity.* If the opponents are on defense for any period of time, they're unable to generate any consistent effective movement. Defensive players usually need the instinctive motivation of ball possession to get fully excited; facing a delay game simply increases their frustration. They get impatient once they do get the ball and often try to catch up all at once to make up for lost time.

2. *To preserve a lead.* Leads melt away in closing minutes even though a team *seems* to be playing the same as before. Tentative offense causes players to keep one eye on the time and have only slight attention reserved for scoring. Every pass, shot, or dribble forces the ball handler to pass self-judgment on each act. Such judgment creates tightness and this tightness results in a lack of fluidity that once existed earlier in the game.

A new offensive style such as a delay game is a must in order to create the attitudinal change necessary to keep playing and trying to score with authority.

3. *To earn a last shot for any quarter or half.* This situation is a form of delay game to be used when the score is either tied or we are leading. We work very hard at sending our opponents off the court after they've just been scored on with a well-executed maneuver. It becomes a strong psychological weapon.

4. *To capitalize on the foul and bonus situation.* Our delay game allows our players in foul trouble to remain in that game for a longer period. (It could also help an opponent who is in foul trouble so the coach must know foul numbers on everyone.) This may also apply to the latter stages of the first half as well as the second half. If we can't afford a player's temporary absence (especially our big man), we delay to play less defense.

If we have more fouls than they do, we'll sometimes delay to catch them up to us and put us into the bonus situation. If they are already in foul trouble, we'll delay ... especially if we're shooting the bonus.

There are certain delay principles that we stress repeatedly. They apply specifically to the Penetration's delay games but could equally pertain to others as well.

DELAY PRINCIPLES

1. *The delay offense should be similar to the regular offensive set.* We try to keep our players in their natural positions whenever possible. A change in offensive alignment is like a red flag waved in front of a charging bull. The defense feels that the change in alignment is a signal that the offense doesn't want to penetrate any more.

It may be an advantage for certain teams to conceal their real offensive intentions from fans. On the road, a delay may create a subconscious sympathetic impact on the officials.

If at home, certain groups of fans (who are ignorant of the rules and/or intended strategy) may actually boo their own teams or coaching staff. This may create confusion in the player's minds.

2. *The delay must activate all players and the ball.* Both the players and the ball must be kept moving. This effectively stops the defensive pressure from reforming once temporary offensive penetration occurs. The players must keep active so that they're always receiving passes while traveling toward them. The set must realistically entertain all five defenders so no two are ever brought to the ball. If all players keep moving, they won't "stiffen up" either physically or emotionally. Stiffening would cause them to lose their game timing and rhythm. This loss will then carry over into the defensive attack.

3. *The delay must create open driving lanes for quick penetration.* Such lanes aren't necessarily scoring lanes. It's demoralizing to the defense to have a dribbler penetrate all the way to the basket, not shoot, and then continue dribbling out the other side.

These lanes must be as vertical as possible. Such positioning creates many options of downscreens away from the ball. Such screens effectively create brief offensive mismatches and quick scores.

4. *The delay must keep offensive and defensive floor balance.* The offense must spread the defense. This extended spacing prevents defenders from effectively playing the ball and man together. Like all offenses, defensive balance must be provided to cover up in case of a turnover or missed shot.

5. *The delay attack must be versatile enough to incorporate certain player skills.* We must make room for our most confident and competent ball handlers and foul shooters. Our two best rebounders must be inserted into the attack, but only for specialized purposes. Their ball-handling chores are minimal yet they're often used as release valves

for the ball. They must help to spread the lane to open vertical routes yet be close enough to score off missed shots or inside drop-off passes.

The delay game, like all offenses, has its drawbacks. Coaches must be aware of them and guard against them happening. However, informing the players of these feelings may produce a self-fulfilled prophecy. The adage "paralysis through analysis" could cost that coach an occasional win.

If a team plays their delay game as a keepaway contest rather than as an honest scoring attack, they are doomed for some losses. They'll probably still beat most weak teams but will have problems when the tougher clubs arrive.

If a delay team plays too slowly, this could allow an inferior team to stay too close. The team with less talent will then have reduced time with the ball. This minimizes possession mistakes. The longer the weak team stays close, the more confidence they develop as the game progresses.

A delay game can also backfire if a team slows down the pace so that it unknowingly aids an opponent. For example, if an opposing team has "star" players that are either injured or sick, they'd be unable to physically keep up with a fast-paced game. A delay game would accommodate such a handicapped player.

Lastly, a delay game is sometimes tough to run against a strong pressing team. To control this game's tempo, the delay team must first break presses successfully.

WHEN TO DELAY

Coaches use two basic methods to decide when a team should run their delay attack. Some coaches stick faithfully to one or the other, while others combine both approaches.

The first choice is to rely on the "seat of the pants" approach. Many coaches effectively depend on their experience of past games and instinctively decide, "it's time!"

The second plan is to depend on available game data to reach a decision. If certain levels of time and score exist in a particular game, the delay is ordered.

Other coaches seek more game information before deciding to delay. Such additional factors are listed below and are all crucial when using delaying tactics:

1. Which players on both teams have three or more fouls each?
2. How many time-outs are remaining for each team?

3. Which of the teams are in the bonus situation?

4. Is the game home or away?

Some coaches may choose to play the percentages a little more closely. It's sometimes too much to ask a coach to keep in mind all the game's statistical data and then glean from it whether he should delay or not.

I've devised a simple chart that can be checked quickly when delay time is near. The chart reduces the delaying decision to pure math. It takes into account only the point spread and remaining minutes. The form is best kept on a handy 3″ x 5″ index card and kept in the coach's pocket.

Diagram 7-1 shows the Delay Time-Point Chart. The minutes remaining and present point spread are arranged vertically in two adjacent columns. When the coach considers the delay, he draws an arrow through the time left on the clock and then through the present point spread going from left to right.

If the arrow is exactly *horizontal*, it is usually safe to delay. If the arrow goes *downward* from minutes to points, it is usually very safe to delay. If the arrow goes *upward*, it's generally not a good time to begin the stall.

Delay Time-Point Chart

Minutes	Points
0-59	3+
1-1:59	4+
2-2:59	5+
3-3:59	6+
4-4:59	7+
5-5:59	8+
6-6:59	9+
7-7:59	10+

DIAGRAM 7-1

The chart is based on the theory that the delaying team can lose one point per minute for the rest of the game and still win the game with a two- or three-point margin.

Arrow A shows the team up five points with between two and

three minutes left on the clock. It's safe to delay in this situation as the arrow is horizontal.

Arrow B shows between five and six minutes left with a six-point lead. This is a questionable time for the delay.

Arrow C shows the team up by nine points with between three and four minutes left. This is a very good opportunity to go with the delay.

If these cards are used and then kept after each game, some revealing delay information would be available. Such actual game data could tell whether a coach should stick with the chart as is or adjust the figures.

If you still question whether to delay or not, you might want to consider the following factors:

1. *The time-out factor.* If the delaying team has more time-outs left than their opponents, they can avoid five-second, closely guarded calls by using the time-out. Additionally, a quick time-out can be called after the score to set up the press.

2. *The bonus situation.* The delaying team's chances of winning improve once they begin shooting the bonus free throws. Conversely, if their opponents are not shooting the bonus, they can confidently delay and know that they can waste some fouls and not send their opponents to the foul line.

3. *The game's location.* You should use the delay earlier at home than on the road as the home crowd can be a positive factor on the official's judgment.

4. *The individual foul problem.* Strong consideration must be given to the number of players from each team that have either three or four personal fouls. Defensive players with four fouls are hesitant to foul (even in a strategic fouling situation) during the last minute of play.

After using the Time-Point Chart and a quick analysis of the above factors, you can decide when to delay on a consistent basis.

FOUR LEVELS OF THE DELAY GAMES

We use four basic levels, or degrees, of the delay game. This breakdown includes four separate delay-type offenses which all serve different purposes. They will now be covered in detail.

Level 1: Play for One Offense

We use this form of delay game when we want the last shot attempt of each period if the conditions are good. Although it's not a pure delay, it is a set offense with a deliberate purpose in mind. Many teams don't play for one shot intelligently. They put up any shot with little regard for timing, rebounding, or general organization.

This offense is run when we're leading or tied with usually less than a minute remaining in the period. We may score, miss the shot, or even get fouled. The least we expect is that if we do miss it's of neutral benefit and really can't hurt us.

Our "One" Offense can also be used either as a stall or as a means of isolating a defender in foul trouble. It opens up the lane for driving by our best one-on-one player. "One" constantly sends cutters toward the ball with strong backdoor opportunities if they are being strongly denied.

It also keeps our big man away from the ball during these cuts yet incorporates his assets during the actual last shot.

Diagram 7-2 shows the initial player alignment when we "go for One." It is a right-handed offense that we devised to play to our strength.

Wing 4 is our best one-on-one player who is good at freeing himself of defenders in order to receive passes. It is also helpful if he is a consistent foul shooter.

Player 5 is our big man who is near the left hash mark. This position near the trailing official allows him to call the emergency time-out if we need it.

Our 1, 2, and 3 players are our guards who rotate in a triangle with lane flashes and cuts. They do the bulk of the passing and ball handling. Guard 1 is high above the top of the key; 2 is on the low left block; 3 begins on the short-wing position on the weak side.

The "One" Offense begins with the ball at guard 1. Player 4 gets free on the wing and receives 1's pass as shown in Diagram 7-3. Player 1 cuts through the lane after setting up his defender with a V-cut and then executing a face cut between the ball and his defender.

Player 1 hesitates briefly at the ballside block, looking for 4's pass. He then quickly crosses the lane to replace 2. Player 3 flashes briefly toward the lane and then cuts up high toward the top of the circle. Player 4 passes to 3 as soon as possible.

Player 2 has replaced 3 in the short wing as 3 has replaced 1 high above the top of the circle.

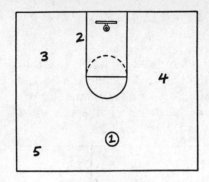

DIAGRAM 7-2
One Set

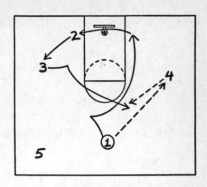

DIAGRAM 7-3
One Offense

If 4's defender pressured 4's pass to 3, then 4 may be open for his own backcut and bounce pass from 3.

The offense continues with 3's return pass to 4 and subsequent cut through the lane as 1 previously did.

If any of the 1, 2, or 3 cutters find themselves denied their flash to the top of the key, it is the signal for them to quickly backcut looking for 4's pass.

We usually go into the "One" Offense with less than one minute left before the end of the period. It is signaled by raising the index finger and saying "Play for One!" The "One" rotation continues until there are 12 seconds left in the end of the period. At 12 seconds, we send our big man 5 to the ballside block to set a baseline screen on the ball side.

This sets up our "Six" shot. We call it "Six" as the shot is ideally taken with six seconds left. This time period gives us one shot plus a chance for one or two second shots. There is not sufficient time for the opponents to go full-court and score.

Wing 4 then returns the ball to the available point man at the top of the key. After his pass, 4 cuts to the baseline and uses 5's screen as he cuts through the lane to the weak side.

The weakside wing pinches down low with the weakside block player to form the double screen as 4 cuts around it for the point's swing pass and short jump shot.

Big man 5 covers the weakside boards. The point guard steps to the foul line for a quick rebound. He's also responsible for the defense against a break should a long rebound develop. The chances for such a long rebound, however, are slight as 4's jump shot is only from about ten feet from the basket.

The last shot just described is shown in Diagram 7-4.

The options from the "Six" shot are few and simple. If 5 sees that the point guard is unable to deliver the ball to 4 around the double screen, he must flash toward the point guard for a short lane jumper or set a screen for the point guard as he drives right for a short jumper. These two options are shown in Diagram 7-5.

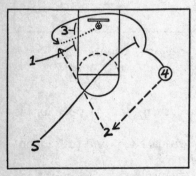

DIAGRAM 7-4
"Six" Shot

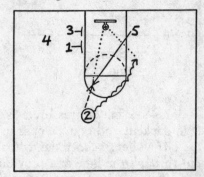

DIAGRAM 7-5
"Six" Options

Level 2: Take a Minute Offense

This offense is designed to take some time off the clock—yet not so it's noticed. We run our normal offensive pattern against our opponent's defense but won't take a shot until the present minute digit on the scoreboard is reduced by one. We don't wish our intention to be known, so subtlety is needed in the bench signal.

When we call "*Take* him," "*Take* good shots," "*Take* your time," or any other suggestion using the word "Take," it means we want to *Take* that minute off the clock. If the clock reads 6:45 and we give the "Take" signal, this means we will continue to run our regular offense but not shoot until the clock reads 5:59 or less. To avoid the players' constant watching of the clock we yell "Good job!" when the digit has changed. We'll obviously shoot a lay-up (if one is offered earlier) but want to stick to our plan to "Take a Minute."

The Take a Minute Offense has often been enough to win many games without resorting to the third or fourth levels of our delay game. Inevitably, more obvious delay levels must be run to win the tougher games.

Level 3: Elbow Delay Offense

As stated earlier, we run our primary delay offense from our original 2-2-1 set. We use it to temporarily disguise our delay plans. The players are all confidently operating from positions of familiarity.

The Elbow Delay was taught to me by one of my assistant coaches. This knowledgeable coach, Roger Lemenager, led New Bedford High School, in Massachusetts, to the 1961 Class A state title.

The Elbow Delay is shown in Diagram 7-6. Guards 1 and 2 line up in the normal 2-2-1 spots as forwards 3 and 4 occupy both high posts in the elbow area. We insert an extra ball-handling quick guard into the low 5 spot. The Elbow is mirrored to run both ways because guard 5 can begin on either low post position. As soon as the ball is passed from guard to guard, 5 must get to the weak side away from the ball.

An underlying strategy for placing both forwards high is to stabilize the two strongest and most aggressive defenders in that critical area. The defenders' desire for steals will work against them as the offense develops.

The Elbow Delay starts after the first guard to guard pass, as shown in Diagram 7-7. After 2 passes to 1, he cuts off post 4. He can go either over or behind 4. If he gets no pass, he headhunts for 5's defender in the lane. Player 5 jab steps toward the lane and comes up high around 4 looking for 1's pass and short jumper. We really don't want this shot but hope to convince the defense we've just altered our attack but are still looking to shoot.

After 2's low screen, he crosses the lane to the other low post and awaits a screen on that side.

The rotation continues as 1 passes to 5 (who has replaced 2 as the guard). Player 1 also cuts either high or low over post, 3 looking for a return pass, and then down to headhunt 2's defender on the low post. This is shown in Diagram 7-8.

There are two scoring options that can develop once the defense starts to anticipate the Elbow's movements.

The first occurs when the two aggressive post defenders begin to come up high looking to steal the guard-to-guard pass. When this happens, it presents an easy backdoor pass from the guard to the forward whose man attempted the steal. This first automatic option, our Post Back, is shown in Diagram 7-9.

Guard 2 passes to 1, runs off 4's screen, and sets his screen low on 5. Player 5 comes from behind the post screen and X4, in going for the

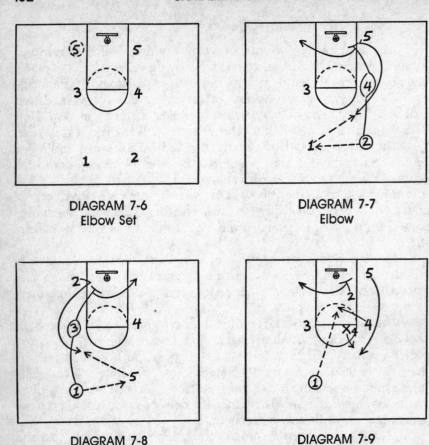

DIAGRAM 7-6
Elbow Set

DIAGRAM 7-7
Elbow

DIAGRAM 7-8
Elbow Rotation

DIAGRAM 7-9
Post Back

steal of 1's pass, temporarily loses defensive contact with post 4. Post 4 then backcuts to the open lane area as 2 has cleared to the ballside low post. Player 4 should have one dribble and a power lay-up. This is a very effective scoring move against post overplay.

The second productive scoring option is the Guard Cross, as shown in Diagram 7-10. Player X5 may try to get over 2's approaching downscreen and slide up the lane slightly while anticipating 5's cut. When 5 reads his defender's cheating move, he crosses the lane for a lob pass from guard 1 and a quick score.

These two options serve well to reduce overplay. Their effectiveness in scoring obviously increases the Elbow's delaying efficiency. It's truly a delay but also doubles as a strong scoring attack. We accomplish all the delay objectives without the obvious spread offenses that require special personnel who must penetrate and make big free throws.

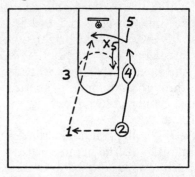

DIAGRAM 7-10
Guard Cross

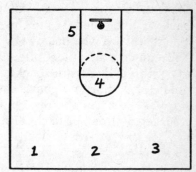

DIAGRAM 7-11
Three Corner Set

Level 4: Three Corner Lay-Up Offense

We turn to our Three Corner Lay-up Offense when we need a change of pace in the last two minutes of a game that we're winning. Some coaches refer to such an offense as a *freeze*, but we really try to score from it. As the name implies, we want lay-ups, and the only other shot we'll take is the free throw.

This offense has the advantage of resembling a dribbling stall, but when the defense gets lazy and figures we're not looking to score, it quickly becomes a potent scoring attack.

Diagram 7-11 shows the beginning alignment of the Three Corner Lay-Up Offense. Our three best ball-handling guards are lined up just over the midcourt line with 3 having the ball.

Forwards 4 and 5 are in the lane area. Forward 4 is just above the foul line and 5 is on the left low post. The offense is geared for right-handed guards on the vacated right side but it's helpful if either 4 or 5 is left-handed. The whole side is cleared out for the guards' penetration to the lane and a lay-up.

The Three Corner begins with the guards across the time line holding the ball until the opponents have picked up man-to-man.

When this is done, guard 3 drives the right side looking to score a lay-up. Most defenders will "fan" the dribbler to the outside. This usually presents a change-of-direction dribble once the guard is below the free throw line extended with a good chance for a lay-up.

When 3 reaches the baseline and has no shooting opportunity, he can do one of two things: keep dribbling through the lane and come out the other side, or pass backward to 2, who has filled his spot on the right sideline. Player 3 always goes through the lane and comes back out the other side to the midcourt line and replaces 1. Player 1 has filled for 3 who has by now started his drive down the right side. This can continue indefinitely as the three guards keep dribbling on the right and passing backward to the next guard to repeat the procedure. After any guard has gone through and come up the left side, he becomes the next player most responsible for calling the emergency time-out to the trailing official.

As the guards run their penetrating moves, high forward 4 screens low for post 5 who replaces him up high. The high forward is always responsible for continuing to flash toward a guard in trouble to serve as a safety valve. Once the guard begins his dribble, however, the high forward goes low (this is timed with the guard's dribbling penetration) to screen for his weakside forward. They exchange on the ball's penetration. This is shown in Diagram 7-12.

There are two popular defensive stunts our opponents attempt when combating the Three Corner Lay-up Offense. The first involves the ball being trapped with the defensive guard coming from behind. This is easily solved by the back guard orally warning the ball handler of the impending trap. There are then at least two release passes available out of the trap as shown in Diagram 7-13. Either of the two back guards will be open. After the pass out, the guard with the ball continues the dribbling rotation as the front guard crosses the lane.

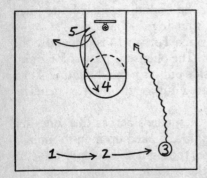

DIAGRAM 7-12
Three Corner Offense

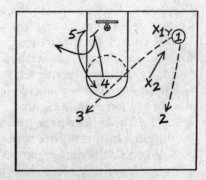

DIAGRAM 7-13
Trap Release

The second maneuver designed to disrupt the flow of the Three Corner involves the defensive forwards guarding 4 and 5. As they screen for each other, the post defenders switch automatically on each downscreen. When this occurs, the low forward crosses the lane (before the switch) and looks for the guard's short pass and a lay-up. This is shown in Diagram 7-14. This little move has given us many easy baskets during the final minutes of numerous games, but it works best when the defense has had adequate time to study the Three Corner's movement and they anticipate the forwards' screening routes.

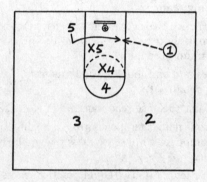

DIAGRAM 7-14
Low Cross

COACHING GUIDELINES FOR THE DELAY GAME

1. Have as a game goal the limiting of four team fouls going into the fourth period. If you can stop at four fouls, you can get the ball immediately after their free throws following your next foul, rather than not having enough fouls to have them shoot the bonus.

2. When delaying, the pressure is on the defense ... not the offense.

3. The delay game must be practiced ... talk and diagrams aren't enough.

4. When ahead in the closing minutes, have your best offensive players on the court. When losing at the end, play your strongest defensive players.

5. During time-outs, limit yourself to three separate units of information, repeat them, and them send them out on the floor.

6. Make sure your players always know the following five late game facts:

    a. The defense they are to return to.

    b. The five second closely guarded rule.

    c. The number of time-outs remaining.

    d. When your time-outs should be used.

    e. The two top opponents that should be fouled if necessary.

7. Begin the Three Corner Lay-up Offense practice period by going against the poorest defensive players on the team. Then proceed to playing against six defenders once confidence is established. Put a penalty on the defense if they don't come up with a steal within a definite period of time. Allow the defense to foul in order to upset the delaying team.

8. Always practice two of the delay offenses the day before each game. Drill them in short time segments as this gives maximum repetition and minimum boredom.

9. Bad passes and bad shots are bad mistakes. They should be charted and then penalized.

10. Have a "junk" defense ready for end-of-game situations.

11. Develop your team's tempo control on a game-by-game basis. Don't marry a tempo for a full season if you won't be happy with it during each game.

12. Divide your team into two equal practice teams for varying levels of your delay games. Have a mini-scrimmage of four minutes during each practice. Keep a won-loss record of each team over the complete season. Chart the games and do a mini-sports report for the bulletin board. All names and actions that are mentioned must be described with a positive flavor.

13. Experiment with a special delay team that can confidently deliver in games. They may not always be your best game players. Apply pressure to this mini-team in practice sessons so that they are accustomed to facing handicaps.

CHAPTER 8:

Blitzing with the Penetration's Fast Break

Imagine this ... you're playing at home against your big rival in a close game. Each teams' points have been well-earned through hard work and extra effort. Both the crowded bleachers and those standing on the sides have modestly cheered during the game while commenting, with sophisticated terms, on each set play's finer points.

Suddenly, your fans are spontaneously brought to their feet (later they wondered how they got up). The crowd is applauding as an audience will naturally do following some instant excitement. They are wildly punching the air and slapping their neighbors' backs while creating a wave of thunderous bedlam seldom heard during winter months. It is such a blur of sound that no one person can be singled out.

The players below are backpedaling on defense and crediting each other for a great play's success.

What occurred on the court that could so quickly transform seated parents and friends into a standing mob of cheering fanatics?

The answer is really simple ... a group of five players just combined all their talents into an electrifying full-court attack that resulted in a fast-break basket.

Many fans see such scoring and assume it is nothing but accidental offense by highly talented players. The opposite is usually true. Many teams of average skills are able to score consistently using the breaking game but only through constant organization and practice. Most teams are able to score the easy basket via the fast-break route if the running game's concepts are understood and applied by the players.

A brief set of reasons for running the break follows. These are the highlights of the fast break and will be emphasized repeatedly to the squad as they occur in games and practice situations.

WHY THE FAST BREAK?

1. The Fast Break Creates Offensive Problems for the Opponents

a. Opponents can't gang up on their offensive boards; some must stay back to protect against the long threat.

b. Teams must run a more deliberate, tentative attack knowing that a turnover or missed shot will result in a quick fast-break score. The breaking team then dictates game tempo.

c. Opposing teams must devote valuable practice time to combat the upcoming opponent's breaking game.

2. The Fast Break Creates Defensive Problems for the Opponents

a. The breaking team faces fewer presses due to the full-court familiarity. They have great lane recognition.

b. It negates the surprise of multiple defenses.

c. The court area from the foul line to the basket is much tougher to guard by two retreating defenders than it is by five well-positioned defenders set up in their strength. The reduced congestion and forward momentum create more usuable space for scoring maneuvers.

d. It's psychologically tough to run back on defense without the motivation of the ball and the chances of scoring with it.

e. The zone's cycle of popularity is returning due to today's motion offenses, but its weakness against the break is still there. It is reversed as the little players are often the first ones back and the biggest defenders are behind the ball.

3. The Fast Break Makes Physical Conditioning a Game Factor

a. The break demoralizes a team that patiently runs set plays to score, while watching the breaking team then score two quick points.

b. A poorly conditioned or lazy defender will be exploited by the break.

c. The running team's goal is to wear down the opponents in the first half, which makes their defense more vulnerable during the second half.

d. The break builds and maintains a team's conditioning as the season goes on. Players must run with the same speed in the fourth quarter as they do in the first quarter.

e. The running game's numerical advantages increase as the game progresses if the opponents are not in good shape.

4. The Fast Break Is Basketball's Most Natural and Popular Offense

a. Due to its high-powered pace, few players can play the whole game. The bench players, or reinforcements, then get extra playing time. Eight to ten players in each game usually create a happy team.

b. A ballplayer's natural reaction is to attack aggressively when a numerical advantage shows. He can operate from a freedom of play that may be suppressed in a set style.

c. The break is extremely popular with the fans because it generates great excitement and interest. Its stepped-up pace will stand up the crowd and continually put people in the stands. If they boo the stall game, then, conversely, the running game will be cheered.

d. Your genuine enthusiasm for the break is based on your players' developed skill levels. They have learned their fundamentals while moving at top speed. If they play at a fast pace with few turnovers, they can learn to slow down when a game situation dictates. The reverse does not usually apply.

e. You must stress the break and its accompanying teamwork when there is no high-scoring superstar available. If your team has just average talent your team must use the entire court on offense.

f. The coach who employs pressure defense welcomes the break's pressure offense as they complement each other in dominating game tempo.

g. Games on the road are tough to win because few close calls are ever awarded to the visitors. The fast break's ability to score quick unmolested baskets could make a difference in the score.

h. It's the only offense that can quickly overcome a lead.

DISADVANTAGES OF THE FAST BREAK

The fast break has some negative factors that often forces a coach to drop the break from his offense. It must be a total commitment by you if it is going to be foremost in your players' offensive thinking.

Your coaching staff must devote considerable time in the preseason to teaching the disadvantages of the fast break to team members. If they are aware of these factors early and then get reminded when necessary during the season, they are less likely to become severe problems as the season goes on. Once again, your efforts are dedicated toward creating smarter athletes.

My experience has shown that the break's drawbacks are as follows:

1. *The fast break increases turnovers.* One of my pet coaching phrases is "Shots before turnovers!" The break often creates just the opposite as the speed of the players shows up in rushed passes. Players tend to get careless in their desire to hurry. Fast-break turnovers are especially dangerous as the offensive team is usually running the "wrong" way when the turnover occurs.

2. *Your fast break can help a superior team beat you.* The opponents get the ball more often because the break doesn't retain offensive possession for long. This causes more defensive fouling and it then gives the opponents more chances to score. We have actually increased their offensive action situations.

3. *The break can disrupt defensive teamwork.* Some players will "cheat" on their defensive boards in order to run the break prematurely. Additionally, some players may wear themselves out in attempting steals.

4. *The fast break reveals the selfish player.* Individualism tends to surface as the break's structure is less defined and much more emphasis is placed on a player's judgment. The player's acceptance of his game-shooting range often gets extended during the break's excitement. A set offense can often dictate just where the selfish player should get the ball whereas the break cannot.

5. *The break causes many coaches to question themselves.* Some coaches have a love affair with "their" set offenses and may subconsciously reduce the fast break's emphasis in practice or games so that "their" offense can be run. They don't feel that the break is their own offense.

Other coaches can't live with the 15-foot jump shot off the break. If they don't believe in that shot, they don't really believe in the break. The break's up tempo makes this coach unsure about its value.

Many coaches devote much practice time to the break and don't get immediate returns in exchange for the increased early season turnover rate so they drop the break. They then spend the practice time in other areas.

The break also forces you to spend more time on defense in practice. The breaking team's defense must be stronger than the control team's defense because of the additional time spent on defense after the break. Are you willing to spend this extra time on defense?

Before you decide that you want to incorporate the total fast break into your system, you should evaluate your talent in several key areas. You don't have a zoo if you don't have the animals!

Is there sufficient rebounding strength? Can they outlet accurately? How far? Are there two good handling guards who can intelligently run a break? Are they both fast and quick? Can these guards quickly recognize defensive positioning? What type of relationship exists between the coach and his guards? Can they communicate with the coach? Will they reward all of the lane fillers or are there potential cliques that can dull the breaking team? Can they play under control? Is the necessary bench strength available to run the break for a full game?

The Penetration team is position perfect for the fast break. The two guards do the bulk of the ball-handling chores while the remaining forwards rebound, fill lanes, and get into the scoring.

Earlier, the term "total" fast break was used in evaluating personnel. This term is very specific and has deeper meaning. You may have adequate talent to employ a total fast break or because of certain player deficiencies you may choose to run a "limited" break.

A total fast break would include running at the following opportunities:

1. Made field goals
2. Missed field goals
3. Made free throws
4. Missed free throws
5. From defense
6. Violations
7. Jump balls

Again, if your team contains above-average talent, it should consider using all aspects of the total break.

On the other hand, your team may have a "short" bench and just average talent for a given season. If this is the case, you should reduce the breaking opportunities. This may prove to be smart coaching for any combination of the reasons stated earlier as negative break factors.

An example of the limited break would be to drop the made field goal and made free throw break options if your team has confidence in its execution of their press offense. Many teams press after made shots, so why waste valuable practice time on breaking against that setup if you feel really good about using your press attack?

Another team may eliminate breaking after a missed field goal. If they have an exceptionally poor rebounding team, they can't afford to have their guards thinking about receiving outlet passes when they should be helping out on the boards. An exception would naturally occur on a long rebound which would enable a guard to go "solo" full-court.

Teams should always run after an opponent's violation as there is often a brief letdown following this infraction. This moment presents a good chance to attack during their questioning of an official, getting a coach's instruction, or possibly blaming each other.

All teams, regardless of talent, must run from their defense as it is such a natural act. Interceptions, steals, or loose balls are usually followed by much frustration on the ball handler's part. His mistake is usually doubled when he then attacks the ball wildly in an attempt to get it back. This often results in a foul for the defenders.

Whether or not you decide to limit your team's breaking opportunities, you must always execute an early, or, in our case, *Whip Offense* at the end of each trip down the court. This quick-hitting offense, if sound, can capitalize on those few golden moments between the defense's retreat and its final set structure. Big and small defenders are momentarily reversed in a zone, while man defenders in their anxiety to pick up their assigned players are often too close ... especially on the helpside. Such poor defensive positioning makes them vulnerable to flash pivots and other sharp cuts.This defensive confusion, coupled with crisp ball and player movement, could invite a good shot against an unorganized defense. This usually results in poor defensive box-outs that allow multiple shots.

You must decide in which areas you choose to break and then plan a total practice commitment toward these areas. Keep charts to analyze the break's returns and award recognition to those players involved. It is imperative, however, that you, regardless of a total or limited break, have a quick-hitting early attack to explore each time down the court just before the beginning of your set offense. On all possessions, each team must try to squeeze one more breath of life out of the break before resorting to a set offense against a strong and well-organized defense. The Penetration's Whip Offense will be explained later in this chapter.

THE BREAK'S MENTAL STATE

A successful breaking team is comprised of defenders who are break conscious. To a great extent, the team's conversion time from defense to offense is the primary factor in scoring easy fast-break points. Individual players should be so well coached that they can react to all running situations without hesitation.

When ball possession is gained, your players should have one thought … to score as quickly as possible. Remind them repeatedly to hurry and get into position to shoot without hurrying the shot. Your goal is to advance the ball upcourt as quickly as possible unless you have a time-score factor in your favor. Always stress basketball intelligence and game awareness.

Such consistent use of offensive pressure helps to set game tempo while forcing your opponents to simultaneously think about their upcoming defensive jobs while playing a tentative offense. This overall pressure will search out the one defensive opponent who lets up. Their defense deserves no rest. You hope to limit their rest periods.

WHO CAN PLAY ON A BREAKING TEAM?

All players have varying amounts of court speed and controlled speed. All-out court speed with no body control is of limited value in a running game.

A player may not be a fast player but he can easily be a fine complementary-type player within a fast system. The key to the Penetration's break does not lie in the player's speeds but in the balance and alignment of the personnel. A slower player with great anticipatory skills is more valuable than one with limited functional speed.

TEACHING THE PENETRATION FAST BREAK

For teaching purposes, the court is first divided laterally into three lanes. During all fast-break attempts, these three lanes are filled by all five players.

The *center lane* has as its limits the normal lane lines with their extensions through the center jump circle and finishes at the offensive free throw area. It is always filled by a ball handler and two trailers.

The *wing lanes* are bordered to the outside by the 28-foot hash marks and on the inside by the free throw lane lines and their imaginary extensions over the full-court. There is always one player in each of these two lanes. No players filling either wing lane can be within three feet of the sideline. This limits them to running just *inside* the hash marks and never *over* them. This coaching tip keeps the player far enough from the sideline so he can still remain inbounds while catching an errant pass.

The wing lanes are further designated as either "long" or "late" lanes. This varies depending on which side the outlet pass is released to. The wing lane that receives the outlet pass is considered the long lane because it is usually filled first and contains the player most in front of the ball (or the longest). The late lane is the wing lane filled by one of the three rebounding forwards. Due to their primary responsibility of rebounding first and running last, this lane is often filled after the ball is on its way. This label, however, does not mean that they take part in fewer breaks. In fact, the three-player sprint to fill this late lane often gets the winner out in front of the ball despite his late start. He has no pass-dribble responsibilities and must sprint only to midcourt to do his job.

The players who fill all five areas vary and will be described in detail later in this chapter's development. There is a real emphasis in our fast break with our players learning "principles," not "patterns." The concept is explained as a whole, drilled in parts, and reassembled into a functional tool. It is not an assigned breaking scheme where each player has a set role. It is more of a "happening" where people go to designated areas.

The Fast Break Lane Chart is shown in Diagram 8-1. This concept is taught early in the season using this as a transparency on an overhead projector. All other fast-break teaching charts are utilized the same way.

In addition to the court's division into lateral lanes, it is further reduced into three distinctive vertical phases as the ball advances up the court. They are:

Phase I—Starting Area

Phase II—Fill and Control Area

Phase III—Scoring Area

A brief introduction to each area is necessary for full understanding before an in-depth discussion.

Phase I, or the Starting Area, is the beginning of the fast break where the initial change of ball status usually occurs. It is always the most critical area. Each break's eventual success on the scoring end is usually based on the team's recognition of a running opportunity and its mental quickness in the defense-to-offense conversion time. The limits of this area go from the defensive baseline to the defensive hash marks.

Phase II, or the Fill and Control Area, has as its confines the defensive hash marks up to the offensive hash marks. The Fill area stresses that all five players must fill the available lanes. Once all lanes are occupied, we stress a controlled team speed in the frontcourt. The Control ensures, first of all, a five-man "happening," and secondly, aids their recognition of the retreating defensive structure.

Phase III is the Scoring Area where multiple offensive "waves" strike the defense. The defense has been quickly analyzed and the selected scoring thrusts are directed against it. The objectives in this playoff portion of the break include a high percentage shot, follow-up rebounders, and good defensive coverage if a reverse fast break develops. Its borders begin at the offensive hash marks and end at the far baseline.

Diagram 8-2 shows the Fast Break Area Chart with its appropriate labels.

The Penetration Fast Break will be discussed in detail through all three phases. If, in games, a breaking opportunity develps from a turnover, the principles that govern that specific court area will still be followed.

ALL-POSITION TEACHING OF THE PENETRATION BREAK

It is extremely vital that all of your players learn how to run the break regardless of their size and/or position.

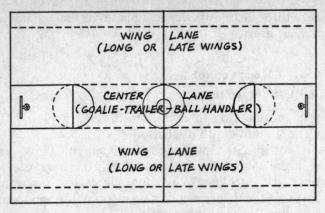

DIAGRAM 8-1
Fast Break Lane Chart

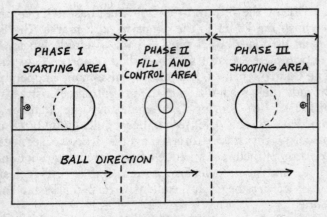

DIAGRAM 8-2
Fast Break Area
Breakdown Chart

Modern passing games and big, agile players do a creditable job of repositioning all defenders. Many teams post guards low while sending big players out to the guard-wing areas to serve as passers. This, of course, sends defenders out there in unfamiliar breaking positions. Because of this, all players must be taught each fast-break role. Unless all players are moderately skilled in all breaking functions, the number of effective fast breaks is reduced.

All players are drilled in all lanes, but we initially teach the break using both guards as outlet receivers and the three forwards as primary rebounders. After the break is introduced and learned by respective positions, we then interchange all positions one by one until total team understanding takes place.

Phase I:
Teaching the Penetration Break from the Starting Area

1. Intelligent defensive pressure stimulates the break.

One of the major requisites for the break is to provide a defense strong enough to force a majority of missed shots. This is not the time for prolonged defensive theory but several points must be mentioned. Regardless of defensive structure, key efforts must be made to achieve the following:

a. Accurately play all passing lanes.

b. Place a lot of pressure directly on the ball.

c. Get the heel of a hand in every shooter's face.

d. Yell "Shot!" on every field goal attempt.

e. Box out the proper rebounding area or player.

2. Defensive rebounding starts most fast breaks.

Coaches often pay a lot of lip service to the rebounding game but provide it little practice time. We all must to a better job of selling this facet of the game to our players.

Whenever two teams play a game of "pickup" basketball, most players have seldom played together. The team that wins, however, is usually the one that controls both boards and is not necessarily the best shooting team.

Defensive board dominance is especially crucial. The offense should be limited to only one shot attempt each time down the court. Two of the best coaching tips to control the defensive boards are to (1) have all players maintain a high-hands position after a shot is taken, and (2) have the nearest defender yell "Shot!" This high-hands box-out stance means that the fingers of both hands are pointed straight up and the elbows are at shoulder height. We stress this for four main purposes:

1. Hands up make it impossible to foul opponents by holding them down low. Insist that the players "Show the ref your hands!"

2. No inside player can effectively pin your player's arms to his sides in an attempt to prevent your team "gathering" with their arms in

preparing to jump. This was the strategy used against UCLA's Lew Alcindor in his early years. Often there are fellow teammates who will accidently do the same thing. Hands up prevents anyone from doing it.

3. Our hands are already up for the shot that misses short off the near rim and comes quickly at the rebounder.

4. The hands-high position also takes up more lateral space, which keeps people further away from the rebounder. This wide stance also enables a player to be a better "traffic"rebounder.

The ball must be ripped out of the air with two hands and held high for maximum protection.

Following this defensive rebound, the rebounder yells "Ball!" No players are allowed to leave their defensive position until they hear this signal. This shout serves well as both a physical and psychological advantage.

The rebounder must try to twist one-quarter of a turn toward the nearest sideline while in the air or immediately upon returning to the floor.

3. Sound outlet passing is crucial to a good start.

The players who can potentially receive the outlet pass must first study the shot to determine at what angle it will come off the board. This early tip allows anticipation as to which guard will receive the outlet pass.

Both guards (or the two players nearest the elbow areas) must each be positioned on the elbow to cut off the long rebounds and act as outlet receivers if a forward rebounds a missed shot. Following the rebound, the ballside elbow player cuts to the free throw line extended into the outlet area. He is the "wide" receiver.

Offside elbow guard immediately steps to the top of the key to serve as a breakaway threat if there is poor defensive balance. He is called the "key" receiver.

The wide receiver can vary his distance up the court as far as the hash mark. He must quickly assess his teammate's capabilities including his ability to throw the long outlet pass and how well he can throw it with varying levels of defensive pressure. The quickness of this pass is more critical than its length. During the early season we put gym tape on the floor to mark the acceptable outlet areas for both rebounders and receivers.

When the wide receiver is in position, he yells his rebounding teammate's name. He makes sure his back is to the sideline, facing in, so that he can see nearby defenders who may try to step in to intercept or draw a charge.

The rebounder keeps two hands securely on the ball following his rebound and outlets to either receiver. The high top pass is released from above the head. Two hands are especially needed as the rebounder can pull back the ball if a defender should step into a passing lane. It is also an accurate pass that can be thrown a long distance without the curving motion that the one-handed "baseball" pass often produces.

The wide receiver must be constantly reminded not to run away from the ball. Breaking upcourt without the ball places great pressure on the passer to throw long and invites defenders to intercept a pass having too much air time. The ball must also be met by the receiver flashing toward it while showing two visible target hands.

Some players may have a tendency to "catch" the outlet pass (or other passes) with one hand by deflecting it to the floor and then dribbling or passing it. We stress that, whenever possible, all passes must be caught with two hands. One hand will usually catch all good passes but one hand won't catch the bad pass. Two hands will surely catch all good and most bad passes.

The two outlet receiving positions are shown in Diagram 8-3. The rebounding forward can outlet either to the wide receiver or to the key receiver.

If both outlet areas are being actively denied, there is a remaining option that can still start a break. The rebounder must "bust out" of the existing defensive coverage used to either delay or smother the initial outlet pass.

This "bust out" is signaled orally by all who see that both outlet receivers are covered. We all yell "You!" This is a strong and direct

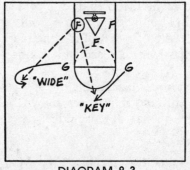

DIAGRAM 8-3
Outlets

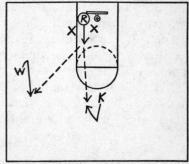

DIAGRAM 8-4
"You"

order for the rebounder to quickly drop low and push the ball with
one hand through the trap to an open area in front for one bounce. He
then chases the ball and will either continue the dribble or pick it up
and pass it to an open player in front.

The "You!" move is shown in Diagram 8-4.

4. Center the ball using both outlet receivers.

Sideline Vs. Center Lane Fast Break

Many good fast-breaking clubs insist on pushing the ball up the
sideline as there is less congestion there giving more rapid ball
advancement. However, the sideline route is often too easily defended
as zoning techniques can effectively stop the longer passing lanes
inherent in that breaking style. If the ball is on the sideline, the
passing options are limited to a centering pass and a crosscourt lob.
Today's players often aren't capable of making such passes accurately
and consistently.

Conversely, when the ball is in the middle during the break, the
ball handler can then reward both lanes with shorter passes than
those needed during a sideline break. Shorter passes mean fewer
turnovers.

The fast break is best executed with the open floor dribble. The
guards must be well drilled in "traffic" dribbling. The ball is only
released to the wings as a last resort when encountering strong
defensive pressure.

Passing Center

Once the ball is cleared from the lane area, it must be quickly
advanced up the floor. The original wide and key outlet receivers (now
designated as "W" and "K") are now responsible for this maneuver.

If the ball is directly outletted to K, he dribbles up the center
lane as W hustles up the long lane in an attempt to get far in front of
the ball. The rebounders are not to outlet directly to K unless they can
see very little defensive pressure and that K has a reasonable chance
of going all the way.

If the ball is outletted to W, he looks to center it using the pass to
K already in the center lane. Both centering moves are shown in
Diagram 8-5 as both W and K approach the fast break's Fill Area.

Dribbling Center

The second method of centering the ball occurs when the wide receiver W gets the outlet pass and is unable to center it to K. The key receiver, K, cuts on an angle toward the far hash mark while looking for W's centering pass. If there is too much traffic and he doesn't receive it, he continues toward the far hash mark while looking for W's centering pass. K has now filled the long lane as W centers himself using the dribble. He may be forced to delay the actual centering move by dribbling in his present lane briefly while trying to force his way into the center lane.

This dribbling center is shown in Diagram 8-6. W can't center to K so he dribbles to the center lane himself. K continues to fill the long lane.

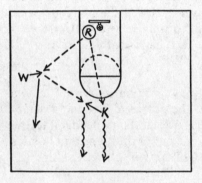

DIAGRAM 8-5
Passing Center

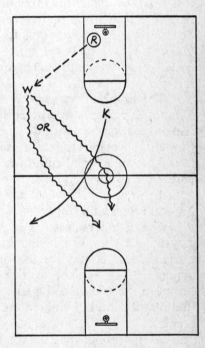

DIAGRAM 8-6
Dribbling Center

This particular phase of the Penetration Break must be perfectly coordinated as both W and K's initial moves make up two-thirds of the break's success. If the ball is centered accurately and the long lane is filled by either player, the chances of scoring quickly are very good.

Phase II:
Fill and Control Area

The Fill Area exists from the defensive hash marks to approximately the midcourt line, and the Control Area continues upcourt to the offensive hash mark boundary.

As the ball is being centered, all five players must be in, or running toward, an area. After the break is underway, one coach focuses on the long and center lanes while the second coach concentrates on the other three players' roles.

The late lane, when filled, completes the first wave of the break. It is filled by one of the three inside rebounders—whoever gets there first. The finish line of this three-player sprint is the midcourt line. The winner keeps hustling to place himself in the ball handler's vision. It is extremely helpful if that person can vocally signal the ball handler just where he is. He may say "Bill, on your right," or "Stay middle, on your left."

The break's first wave of three players is on its way. The two remaining players are crucial to both the potential score and defensive purposes. When the late lane race is over at the midcourt line, the runner-up becomes the trailer who drops out of that lane and hustles into the center lane behind the ball. This row of players behind the ball is called the *Ball Line*.

This trailer must slow down a bit and realize he's in the second wave of attack and can score if he doesn't rush his speed.

The fifth person is the goalie. Once he realizes he'll be the last player down the court, he must also get to the Ball Line in back of the trailer. He must stay on this Ball Line and further back than any opponent. This is done for defensive balance. In case of any quick turnover, the trailer and goalie should be prepared for defense. For this reason, the rebounders are drilled often on defending the fast break.

As the break reaches the midcourt line, all five positions are decided. The players must stay in their earned lanes to eliminate confusion as the break progresses.

Diagram 8-7 shows these areas totally filled as the players approach the Control Area. Wings 2 and 3 run to get in front of the ball as it is dribbled by 1 in the center lane. Trailer 4 is on the Ball Line directly behind 1. Goalie 5 is also on the Ball Line but is further back than any other player.

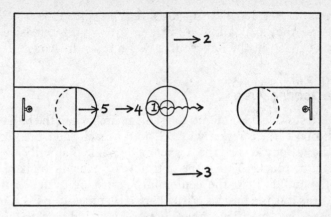

DIAGRAM 8-7
Fill and Control Area

In the Control Area the middle man must reduce and control his speed slightly to allow both wings 2 and 3 to get into his sight, read the defense, and protect the ball.

It is very tempting (especially with young guards) to dribble wildly out of control when sensing an easy two points. Guard 1's split-second delay will allow one or both wings to come into his vision. This concentration on control will expand the team's scoring options.

Additionally, the defense must be analyzed quickly to select the appropriate scoring options on the end of the break. The retreating defenders can present any number of numerical advantages. Some are 1 on 0, 2 on 1, 3 on 1, 3 on 2, 3 on 3, etc. They will all be charted near the chapter's closing ideas. This defensive information being faced must be recognized as soon as possible by the middle man and trailer 4. These numbers must be shouted out so that 1 has a better grasp of the developing situation. To best read the full picture, teach the middle man to bring the rim into his vision. This centers his focus and forces him to see everything in the periphery including all players and the rim.

Finally, the ball must be protected during the final dribbles in this control area. Many defenders, when beaten, attempt a defensive *flick* from behind in an effort to compensate for poor defensive containment. Teach your guards to execute a quick crossover dribble in this area if a beaten defender tries a flick or the trailer warns him of one.

When the ball reaches this area, remind your players, "Control! Control!" so they can allow total lane filling and defensive study. Emphasize speed in the backcourt and poise in the frontcourt.

Phase III:
The Scoring Area

The first wave has entered the scoring area when the ball reaches the hash mark lines. When wings 2 and 3 reach the free throw line extended, they cut toward the basket on an angle that will carry them just above the blocks. This is the optimal angle for the banked lay-up.

Ball handler 1, in the center lane, must be aware of the free throw line as it is the break's critical area. He must drop his hips as he approaches the line. This gives better body balance to his body control and makes him more poised for the proper action. The only way 1 is allowed to penetrate beyond the foul line is if he keeps the ball for a lay-up. By stopping, he can:

a. Check his body momentum to avoid charging after his wing pass.
b. Provide a reliable position from which to swing the ball to the weak side.
c. Serve as a defender against a reversed fast break.
d. Throw an accurate pass from a stationary and controlled position.

After the pass to either 2 or 3, 1 slides laterally to the ballside elbow for a possible return pass and free throw jumper. Notice in Diagram 8-8 that trailer 4 and goalie 5 stay on the Ball Line positions at this stage of the break.

If the wing receiving the ball can't take a shot, he stops without dribbling and waits for the trailer to roll down the lane line with his face cut.

Trailer's Cut

Trailer 4's cut must always begin opposite the first pass. This slashing face cut, beginning on the weak side, sends a cutter (4) in front of the nearest lane defender. He faces the ball at the wing during this cut toward the block while looking for the wing's scoring pass. This is the break's second wave and capitalizes on an unorganized defense.

Diagram 8-9 shows trailer 4's cut down the lane on both the right and left sides. Notice that the weakside wing stays on the block

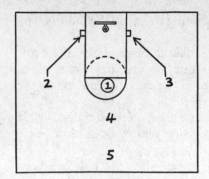

DIAGRAM 8-8
Fast Break's First Wave

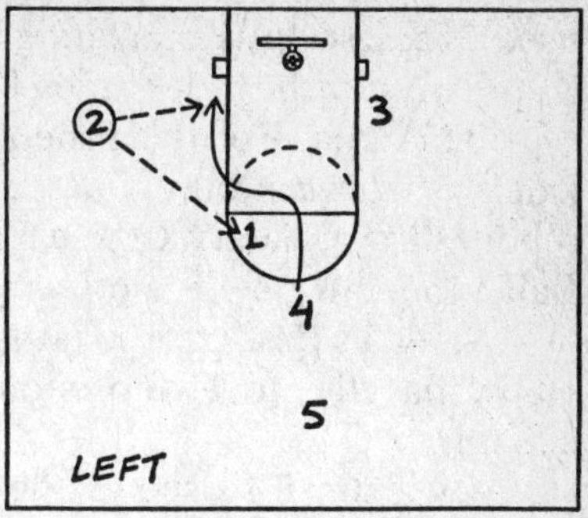

DIAGRAM 8-9A
Trailer Face Cut—Left

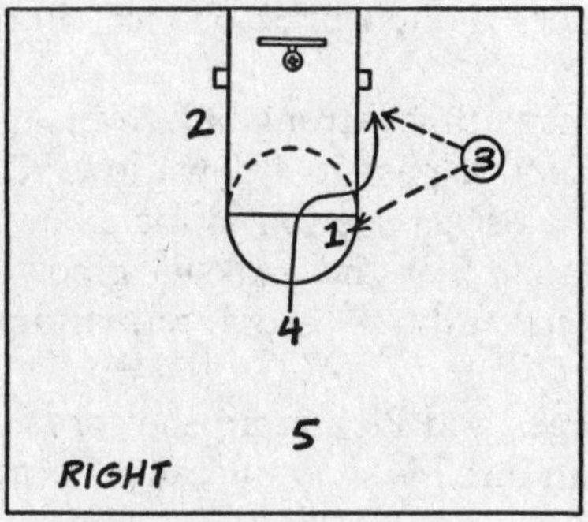

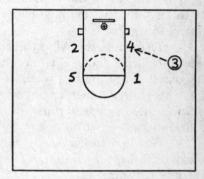

DIAGRAM 8-9B
Trailer Face Cut—Right

DIAGRAM 8-10
Pre-Whip

and middle man 1 steps to the elbow. In addition to being a swing point, 1 also has set a legal backscreen for any retreating defenders trying to stop trailer 4's face cut.

A good variation of the Penetration's fast break is to combine its natural speed and element of surprise with an organized set of plays. The first 90 percent of the break is run the same way, but when it reaches beyond the foul line and no shot has developed, it transforms into a set play offense designed to attack a not-yet-formed defense. This leads to the *Whip Offense.*

Whip Offense

When the trailer's face cut has been run once and no shot results, we flow directly into our early or Whip Offense. The term "whip" is used as a descriptive coaching tool meaning to "whip the ball" (swing it quickly) to the weak side of the floor.

This phase of the Penetration Break changes the goalie's role from what was purely a defensive one to one have a scoring-rebounding capacity. Goalie 5 has trailed the break by staying on the Ball Line, but now the role changes.

After 1's first pass to either wing, goalie 5 steps to the weakside elbow parallel to 1 who is on the ballside elbow. Both elbows are occupied.

Diagram 8-10 shows the pre-Whip set after the ball has been passed to wing 3. Trailer 4 has run his face cut. Offside wing 2 stays on the low post just above the block; 1 has stepped to the ballside elbow; goalie 5 steps to the weak side's left elbow. Wing 3 looks to pass to trailer 4 on the low post above the block as he works for receiving position.

From here the Whip Offense begins with its strong ball reversal and multiple shots. If wing 3 has no shot or pass to 4 down low, he looks to Whip the ball weak side. The safest pass is to 1 at the elbow for his short jumper, or he can skip pass to 5 on the weakside elbow. Such swing passes must be made carefully to avoid retreating defenders.

Goalie 5 can shoot the familiar Pass and Pick jump shot or he can continue the Whip to 2 as 2 pops out into his shooting range for a possible jumper.

Wing 2, after his pop out and reception of the swing pass, may have an excellent driving opportunity here as many weakside defenders overcommit themselves toward the ball in an attempt to stop the shot. This makes them very vulnerable to a quick drive ... especially on the baseline side.

As 2 is popping out, 4 sets a headhunt backscreen on the nearest defender guarding 3. Wing 3 then sets up his defender with a V-cut and continues through the lane toward the low-post area on the ball side looking for 2's pass.

The Whip to this point, with all its options available after one rotation, is shown in Diagram 8-11.

WHIP OFFENSE'S INDIVIDUAL OPTIONS BY POSITION

Wing 3:

1. Shoot.

2. Pass to strongside elbow player 1.

3. Skip pass to weakside elbow player 5.

4. Run lane cut using trailer 4's backscreen.

5. Serve as weakside rebounder, should any shot develop.

Point 1:

1. Shoot.

2. Whip to goalie 5 at the elbow.

3. Skip pass to weakside wing 2 as he pops out.

4. Chase only *certain* rebounds as he is responsible for defense.

Trailer 4:

1. Set legal headhunt screen on wing 3.

2. Roll to near low post facing the ball after the backscreen.

3. Prepare to pop out for the Whip's continuity.

4. Serve as a weakside rebounder.

Goalie 5:

1. Look for skip pass from 3 or relay pass from 1.

2. Take the free throw jumper if open.

3. Swing the ball to 2 as he pops out.

4. Chase *all* defensive rebounds.

Wing 2:

1. Pop out as ball is being whipped to you on reversal.

2. Shoot or drive on any extended defender who is out of control.

3. Look to pass to weakside cutter 3 heading for the low block.

4. Chase all offensive rebounds.

5. Prepare to use 3's backscreen for Whip's continuity if no shot develops.

If no shot develops, the Whip Offense is swung back to the other side, as shown in Diagram 8-12.

Because of the Whip's quick reversal and screening components, it can be run succesfully against either a zone or man defense for several rotations until either a shot develops or a decision is made to go to the set offense.

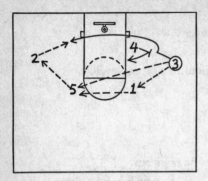

DIAGRAM 8-11
Whip Offense

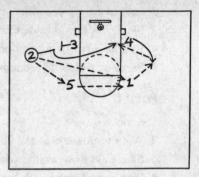

DIAGRAM 8-12
Whip Offense Continued

NUMERICAL FAST BREAK GUIDELINES

As mentioned earlier, all team members must be able to read defenses as they are retreating down the court. Trailers, especially, must help inform ball handler 1 what the defensive picture is. He recognizes the "numbers" and yells them up for all to hear so the first wave of attackers can leave less to chance and can better focus on the familiar task of attacking practiced defensive sets.

He calls up, for instance, "1 on 0," "1 on 1," "2 on 1," "3 on 2," etc. Discuss with your players the numbers and best scoring strategies. This helps your ball handlers' passing judgment and ability to select the correct scoring maneuvers. They mentally know the proper attack for each defensive structure and are better able to transfer it during a game's action.

The following chart provides a much-needed study format from which coaches and players alike can benefit.

DEFENSE FACED	OFFENSE USED	COACHING COMMENTS
1 on 0	Use a banked power lay-up.	1. Teammates must assume the breakaway lay-up will be missed and must actively follow-up all lay-ups.
	Don't shoot over the front rim.	2. Shooter must stay inbounds after lay-up to rebound a possible miss.
2 on 1	Pass first; dribble last.	1. Pepper pass between two players.
		2. Keep about 15' apart to reduce air time of passes.

3. No jump shot allowed. Get either a lay-up or two free throws.
4. Player with ball at top of key must dribble for lay-up to commit defender.

3 on 1	Pepper pass between center lane and wing player. Involve third wing player when in scoring area.	1. "Fool's Gold" or "touch" passes are never allowed from wing to wing across the lane. It's a tempting pass, but it is usually deflected out-of-bounds.
3 on 2 Tandem Defense	Pass early to wing and stay in lanes. Wing shoots short jump shot or swings to elbow.	No "Chump" passes allowed. This is when the ball handler jumps as if to shoot his jump shot and then quickly dumps it down to an unsuspecting wing cutting for an offensive rebound.
3 on 2 Parallel Defense	Keep ball in the center lane as long as possible. Ball handler looks to split the defense, keep the dribble, and shoot the lay-up.	No chump passes allowed.
3 on 3 (or worse)	Delay for break's second wave of trailer and then the Whip Offense.	1. Don't kill the break prematurely ... let it die a "natural death." 2. Trailer must delay his face cut down the lane. 3. Have patience.

Have available many coaching maxims to use during the break; this eases communication between player to player and coach to player. I have broken them up into the three phases of the Penetration Break and also placed them in proper order of sequence that the ball follows from shot score on the other end. Players today don't talk enough ... maybe we should teach them what to say!

Phase I: The Starting Area

1. "Get in his face!"
2. "Shot!"
3. "Hands high!"

4. "Force more missed shots and you'll break more!"

5. "We can break with 60 percent of their missed shots!"

6. "I'd rather have two of you fighting for the ball and lose it than have you both watch someone else get it!"

7. "If you're going to be a spectator ... buy a ticket!"

8. "Get involved on the boards!"

9. "Rip it out of the air!"

10. "Twist away from pressure!"

11. "Get it out!"

12. "Key!"

13. "Wide!"

14. "You!"

15. "Throw the *crisp* outlet pass!"

16. "Catch the outlet pass with two hands and two eyes!"

17. "Center it!"

18. "Be sure of your centering move ... it's better to lose time than lose the ball!"

19. "Go long!"

Phase II: Fill and Control Area

1. "Fill the lanes!"

2. "Beat the ball!"

3. "Sprint!"

4. "How can he beat you? He has to dribble; all you have to do is run!"

5. "Where are the wings?"

6. "Who's long?"

7. "Push it up!"

8. "Bring it!"

9. "Be quick!"

10. "Get in his eyes!" (vision)

11. "Use speed in the backcourt and poise in the frontcourt!"

12. "Call up the defense!"

13. "Watch your spacing!"

14. "Take no more than three seconds between the hash marks!"

15. "Wait for your wings!"

16. "You're too narrow!"

17. "Get wide!"
18. "It's not speed ... it's execution!"
19. "See the rim!"
20. "Get to the Ball Line!"
21. "Chase all breakaway lay-ups. Assume they'll be misses!"
22. "Concentrate on control!"
23. "Two on one? Pepper pass!"

Phase III: Scoring Area

1. "I want to hear your sneakers squeak on those cuts!"
2. "Drop your hips for control!"
3. "Stop at the free throw line!"
4. "Attack before it's (defense) back!"
5. "Slide (step) to the elbow!"
6. "Don't force it ... wait for your trailer!"
7. "Swing the ball!"
8. "Whip it!"
9. "Treat it like a zone!"
10. "Don't overpass!"
11. "Don't dress up your passes!"
12. "Call his name so he'll use your screen for the Whip!"
13. "Shots before turnovers!"
14. "No 'chump' passes, 'fool's gold' passes, or 'touch' passes!"
15. "Don't kill the break ... let it die a natural death!"
16. "Don't cheat the break ... signal me if you're tired!"
17. "We scored ... where were you?"
18. "Bounce pass to score!"
19. "No 'Boys' Club Bounce!" (stationary dribble)

FAST BREAK FROM
FREE THROW SITUATIONS

The free throw situation is a great opportunity from which to run the break. The defense is quite predictable and in a state of flux. It is a retreating zone and the players are, by necessity, reversed by size.

There are four basic times to run off the free throw: (1) a made free throw; (2) a free throw missed right; (3) a free throw missed left; and (4) a free throw missed to the middle. Preparation should be made to cope with each example.

Isolate Set

The first free throw breaking set is called our Isolate Set, as one of our guards is removed from the free throw area.

In the following diagrams, the players will be labeled as follows: 1 and 2 are the guards, 3 is the most mobile forward, 4 and 5 are the two strongest rebounders.

Diagram 8-13 shows the initial set with all players in positions. Guard 1 is on the shooter's left on the lane spot. He will always box-out the shooter by taking one long step beginning with his foot nearest the baseline, and then pivoting to face the basket as he takes the second step with the foot nearest the shooter. He is now facing the basket with the hands-high box-out position mentioned earlier. After this box-out and his contact with the shooter, he spins around upcourt facing his basket and fills the center lane looking for the ball.

Forwards 4 and 5 always position themselves as close to the block as possible. Both feet are placed close together with 90 percent of the body weight on the baseline foot. This makes it easier to swing the "light" foot (nearest the shooter) toward the shooter and at the same time lift up the same corresponding arm. The baseline arm is also raised to the hands-high position to box-out the opponent in the second lane spot. The final position of the two bottom rebounders finds a straight line from baseline foot to lane foot to the shooter. This is the best angle to box-out that second player.

Forward 4 always inbounds the ball as he is going to his right anyway and is often right-handed. This right hand is quicker to release the ball rather than throwing the ball across the body. Forward 5 serves as a safety outlet in 3's previous general area. Forward 4's looks to inbound to 3, 1, or 2.

Guard 2 is at the hash mark on the offensive left serving as an outlet position. He is *isolated*; hence, the name for this maneuver.

Forward 3 starts on the shooter's right. Following the shot, he cuts to the opposite hash mark for an inbounds pass. He waits for a long pass. He'll hold (if no pass) and wait for the ball to be inbounded elsewhere and then fill this wing lane. The ball is centered by either receiver to guard 1, who dribbles quickly upcourt with 3 and 2. Player 5 will be the trailer and 4 is the goalie. Both players must stay on the Ball Line as before.

If the free throw is missed to the right, the break stays the same except that 4 now rebounds and outlets to guard 2 who flashes back toward the ball. Player 2 centers to 1 and they form the first wave with 3 coming in the late wing lane. Player 5 trails on the Ball Line with goalie 4. This is shown in Diagram 8-14.

If the free throw is missed to the left and rebounded by 5, he outlets to cutting 3. Player 4 becomes the trailer and 5 is the goalie. This is shown in Diagram 8-15.

If a long rebound bounces to 1, he may outlet long to 2 going or to 3 as he's cutting by. Player 1 is often able to center it himself by the dribble. Player 5 is the trailer and 4 is the goalie as they both stay on the Ball Line. This is shown in Diagram 8-16.

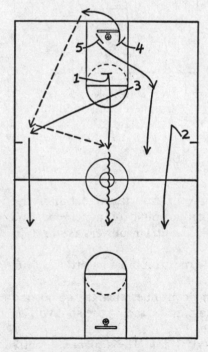

DIAGRAM 8-13
Isolate (Made FT)

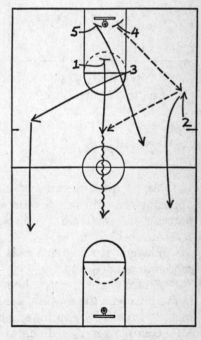

DIAGRAM 8-14
Isolate (FT Missed Right)

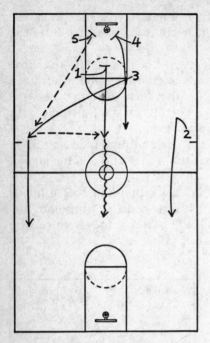 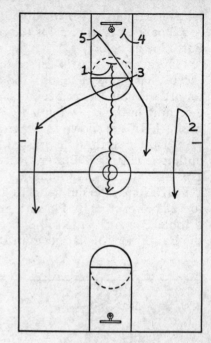

DIAGRAM 8-15
Isolate (FT Missed Left)

DIAGRAM 8-16
Isolate (FT Missed Right)

"Charge" Set

We'll run a second break from the free throw setup if the opposing free throw shooter is either a young or a nervous-type player. This is called a *Charge* play. We line up our players as shown in Diagram 8-17.

Player 1 is the guard as is 2. The most mobile forward is 3. The rebounders are 4 and 5.

Guard 2 checks the shooter and continues straight out of the lane to become the outlet receiver. Forward 3, seeing the shot will be missed, breaks long in his same lane.

Guard 1 serves a different, but vital, role. He is placed directly behind the shooter at the top of the key with loud instructions to look for the charge from the shooter after the free throw attempt. The shooter's coach will often instruct him excitedly to avoid the charge following his shot. Both factors have served many times to create nervousness on the shooter's part to the point of missing the free throw.

Guard 1 then continues to his right to serve as the other outlet receiver along with 2.

Rebounder 4 or 5 outlet the missed free throw to either 1 or 2 depending on which side the shot missed. Whoever receives the outlet dribbles to the center lane as the other player fills the remaining vacant lane. Rebounders 4 and 5 then run their usual sprint for the trailer-goalie contest.

If the free throw is made from this formation, have 5 take the ball from the net and pass long to sprinting 3, short to 2, or diagonally long to 1. The ball then gets centered to 1 in the middle lane as soon as possible. This is shown in Diagram 8-18.

The Charge break is used sporadically, which then forces the coach of the free throw shooter to remind him each time. This creates tension and reduces concentration.

Designate from the bench during each free throw attempt whether you want to run the Isolate or Charge break play.

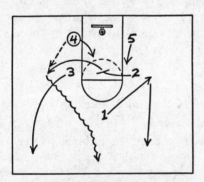

DIAGRAM 8-17
Charge (Missed FT)

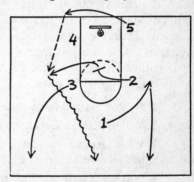

DIAGRAM 8-18
Charge (Made FT)

COACHING GUIDELINES FOR THE PENETRATION FAST BREAK

1. The break must be analyzed concerning your team's individual skills in mind. Drills must be developed specifically for your players' weaknesses or strengths.

2. The progression of these drills should logically fit and lead on to the next.

3. The increase in turnovers will be offset by extra easy scoring. Your players must be reminded of this to maintain confidence during the early season.

4. During games, analyze which side of the court leads to more fast-break scores. Decide why and drill to equalize scoring.

5. When your team scores an easy fast-break basket, it should be followed immediately by a full-court press as panic may ensue.

6. Good descriptive language makes it twice as easy to communicate fast-break terminology to your players.

7. Sell players on the urgency to play the break under control.

8. Insist on pushing the ball up the court before the defense sets up physically, but more importantly, before they set up *mentally*.

FAST BREAK ANALYSIS CHART

If a team makes a commitment to the break, its scoring returns must be constantly evaluated to see if practice time could be better spent in other areas of the game.

The Fast Break Analysis Chart (Diagram 8-19), if kept each game, can be studied on a daily and seasonal basis to see what patterns develop. Practice sessions can then be designed to work on those weaknesses discovered from the chart's study.

Following is a partial list of some fast-break items that can be studied through the chart:

1. Is your team favoring one side of the floor when breaking?

2. Which defense forces the most turnovers?

3. Which team members contribute significantly to the break yet may not show it in other statistics?

4. Is enough patience shown using the break?

5. What areas of the break need more/less practice?

6. What number of fast-break turnovers would also occur on a more controlled type of offensive style?

7. Can your players break more after made field goals or free throws?

8. Are your players in condition to consistently run the break in both halves?

9. Which players are costing you great scoring chances?

10. Who makes turnovers in which areas of the court?

There are numerous other areas of study available for the discerning coach. Increased use of this chart will reveal additional areas. The chart could also be used to analyze your opponent's fast break, which could then pinpoint some of your own weaknesses.

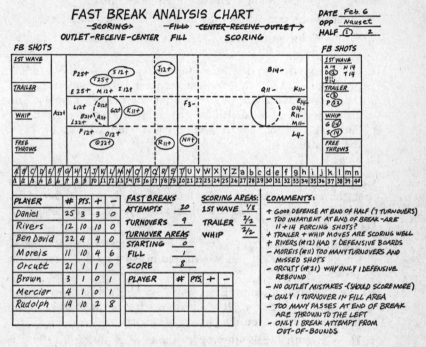

DIAGRAM 8-19

How to Use the Fast Break Analysis Chart

1. Fill in game data in the upper right corner.

2. Draw arrows through the lines above the court diagram showing the ball's direction for that half. (The example shows the ball going from left to right.) If the team were shooting at the other basket, the arrows would be drawn through Scoring, Fill, Center-Receive-Outlet, from right to left in the second line.

3. With each possession, draw a line through the next letter in the alphabet and its corresponding number in the boxes just below the

court. The example shows that T, or 20, fast breaks were attempted in that first half.

4. When a break starts, designate it with the letter, the player's number, and a " + ." Letters are used to distinguish the break attempt from the players' numbers. Show the break attempt as follows:

   a. Defensive rebound—from the area of the thrown outlet pass.

   b. From defense—from area of turnover and circle the letter and the " + ."

   c. Out-of-bounds—from column to left (or right) of the baseline (example: A22 +). An offensive turnover occurring during the break is shown by a " – " sign after the player's number. The possession is also labeled by the appropriate letter (example: F3 –). This means that the sixth break attempt was lost by #3 in the Fill Area.

5. "Finish" the break with the same letter and player's number responsible for the end action. This label is placed on the diagram in the spot the event occurred. The attempted break can be traced by checking what took place with that particular lettered possession. For example:

   a. The first break attempt shows #22 inbounding the ball. It reached the far basket safely but #14 missed his shot on the break's first wave.

   b. The fifth break attempt (E) shows #25 getting a defensive rebound and outletting the ball. It reached the left side where #14 lost the ball on a turnover on the passing attempt.

   c. The sixteenth break attempt (P) shows #25 getting a defensive rebound and outletting safely. The ball reached the scoring end and #22 scored on the trailer play.

   d. The eighteenth break (R) has #11 getting a steal and starting the break. (We know it was from defense because it was circled.) He lost the ball before a shot with a turnover on the offensive right.

   e. The nineteenth break (S) shows #12 getting a steal at the foul line extended area. This break reached the Whip Offense and #14 scored from it.

6. Fill out the player chart in the lower left. Example: Daniel is #25. He received a total of three fast break points. All three were defensive rebounds and outlet passes. This half had no minus points so none was recorded beside his name.

   Moreis (#11) had 4 turnovers (Q,K,R, and M) and two misses from the break's first wave.

7. Complete the total statistical information just below the court

diagrams. From it the following facts are seen:

There were 20 fast break attempts (A through T).

There were nine turnovers (F, B, Q, K, E, O, R, M, and L). These areas, with their contained turnovers, are easily counted as the court is divided conveniently using the dotted lines.

The Scoring Areas are listed on both sides of the court and are divided into first wave shots (1/8), trailer shots (2/2) and "Whip" shots (2/2).

There were no free-throw fast breaks attempted.

8. Under "Comments" designate each item with a plus or a minus to show strengths or weaknesses.

Save all charts to glean such information as team/player characteristics that may repeat themselves during the season.

Beat the Ball Drill (Diagram 8-20)

WHY: 1. To practice outlet passing and centering against defensive pressure.

2. To fill the late lane quickly enough to beat the ball upcourt.

HOW: 1. Coach (C) is at the top of the key. He signals to D (who has the ball) which side the coach wants the ball tossed off the backboard. D is the only one of the four players allowed to see the coach's signal. Both guards must be alert as neither can anticipate which will be the wide or key receiver.

2. D tosses the ball off the board and R rebounds. R twists to outlet the ball to either the wide or the key receiver as D applies token defense. The key receiver must avoid the coach during his cut. The coach plays a passive defense in the center lane.

3. The ball gets centered as soon as possible. D now hustles downcourt to fill the vacant late lane. His job is to beat the ball by the time he reaches the scoring area.

4. The three lanes of the break's first wave are filled as the ball must be brought to the foul line before being passed to either of the two wings.

5. Rebounder R runs downcourt as a single defender. He can break up the scoring attack by merely *tagging* any player with the ball before the shot. Any R who earns a "tag" gets excused from the team's next sprint drill.

6. The next four players step on the court as the four who just ran the drill return and fill different roles.

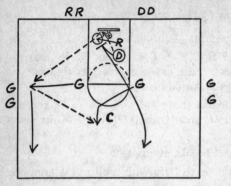 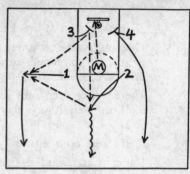

DIAGRAM 8-20   DIAGRAM 8-21

Outlet and Center Drill (Diagram 8-21)

WHY: 1. To practice the two-handed top outlet pass.
            2. To practice receiving outlet passes from both the wide and key areas.
            3. To fill all three lanes quickly and to score at the other end.

HOW: 1. Guards 1 and 2 line up with forwards 3 and 4 in the four lane corners as shown in Diagram 8-21.
            2. Manager (M) in the lane puts the ball off the board as 3 or 4 rebound and outlet to guards 1 or 2 in either the wide or key positions. M gives token defense to outlet passer.
            3. The ball gets centered by either a pass or a dribble and all four players run the break. The nonrebounding forward must beat the ball downcourt in the late lane as the first wave scores against no defense.
            4. After a group of four players run their break, they pick up the jump ropes out-of-bounds on the baseline and jump while waiting for the rest of the team to finish their turns. After this, a different group of four run the break the other way.

TIPS: 1. Gradually add defenders. First, add a lane defender. Next, add a top of the key defender. Finally, add a second lane defender.
            2. Utilize the trailer's face cut once the third defender is added. Until then, the trailer must stay on the Ball Line.

4-3-2-1 Drill (Diagram 8-22)

WHY: 1. To practice all basic fast-break numerical advantages, such as the 4 on 3, 3 on 2, 2 on 1, and 1 on 0.
            2. To practice defensive fakes.

HOW: 1. Players 1, 2, and 3 are the first wave of a fast break with 4 as a trailer. They attack defenders 5, 6, and 7 as they begin the drill while lined up at the midcourt line (a).

2. The 5, 6, and 7 defenders can't cross the midcourt line until the ball reaches the hash marks. This gives the offense a realistic defense in transition.

3. After the 4 on 3 attack (use the trailer), the three defenders 5, 6, and 7 attack the two middle players, 1 and 4, of the previous attack. They go for the other basket. Defenders 1 and 4 must mix up their parallel or tandem defensive styles to force the offense to select the right scoring options. The middle man with the ball must always stop at the foul line.

4. Following the 3 on 2 attack, defenders 1 and 4 must run a 2 on 1 attack going the other way against middle man 5. They must run the pepper pass as often as possible. If one of the offensive players should break away completely from 5, his offensive teammate must stay with the play assuming his teammate with the ball will miss the lay-up. They are reminded that a breakaway lay-up should always be banked off the side and never taken over the front rim.

5. After a player gets done, he goes to any spot out-of-bounds on any sideline to step into any of the 1-7 spots ... whatever is vacant. All players must practice all roles in the drill.

3 on 2 Plus Chaser Drill (Diagram 8-23)

WHY: 1. To fill the lanes quickly with all players getting the chance.
2. To produce the quick shot without hurrying or overpassing.

HOW: 1. There are two evenly talented teams—the "A" team and the "B" team. Three "B" players line up at midcourt with the middle man having the ball. Two "A" players are near the hashmark area to defend the 3 on 2 break. Both teams must alter their two-man defense between tandem and parallel to aid the offense's recognition.

2. These teams not active are out-of-bounds on opposite sidelines.

3. The "B" team on offense attacks two retreating "A" players. When the ball reaches the top of the circle, an extra "A" defender runs onto the court as a defensive chaser to bother the breaking team. He must first touch the inside of the center circle and then he can help his two defending "A" teammates. The next two "B" players on the sideline go to play defense for the next attack of "A" players.

4. Following this 3 on 3 attack, the three "A" players run a three-lane break against the two "B" defenders.

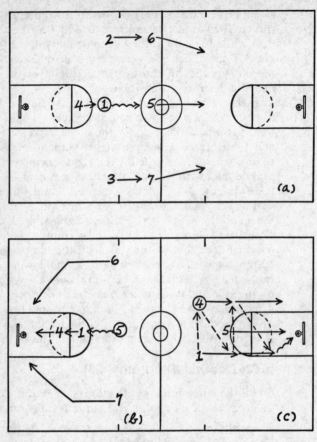

DIAGRAM 8-22

5. When the "A" attack pushes the ball into the free throw circle, this signals the third "B" as a chaser to help his teammates defend the 3 on 2 fast break. If the offense wastes any time overpassing, the break is very quickly changed into a 3 on 3 game.

6. The drill continues up and down as a 3 on 2 fast-break attack. When players get through their active role in the drill, they hustle to the end of their respective team's line out-of-bounds at the sidelines and await their turn to be active as defenders, chasers, and lastly, as attackers.

7. The drill ends when one team scores ten baskets or some other figure designated by the coach.

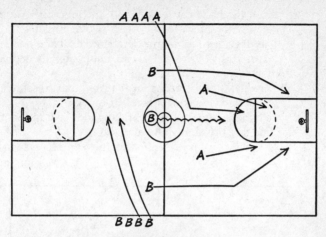

DIAGRAM 8-23

Four to Score Drill (Diagram 8-24)

WHY:
1. To attack quickly and under oncoming strong defensive pressure.
2. To develop a delaying defense when faced with a fast break.
3. To provide solid team competition with scoring as motivation.

HOW:
1. Divide the team into three equally talented mini-teams designated as "A," "B," and "C."
2. The "A" team has the ball centered at midcourt with both wing lanes filled and a trailer on the Ball Line.
3. The "B" and "C" teams each have two defenders near the top of the circle and two more waiting out-of-bounds at the hash marks. The two defenders on the court must, again, switch their defensive alignment between parallel and tandem. The diagram shows "B" as the team defending "A" team's attack and the "C" team is waiting in the backcourt.
4. When the "A" team's 4 on 2 attack reaches the top of the key, this signals the two "B" defenders out-of-bounds at the hash marks to rush in to help defend against the "A" team's attack. Unless the "A" team scores quickly, a 4 on 4 situation develops. It is especially vital that the trailer's face cut be brought into the attack.
5. Once the four "B" players get the ball (after a score, rebound, turnover, etc.), they attack the two "C" players on the other end of the court with their own 4 on 2 break. Again,

when the ball reaches the foul line area, the two extra "C" defenders rush in to help their two teammates.

6. The previous "A" team members await the oncoming "C" team. Two players must wait out-of-bounds near the hash marks.

7. This drill emphasizes that it takes "four to score"; i.e., the trailer must make his face cut quickly or the two hustling defenders coming from out-of-bounds will nullify any one-time fast-break advantage.

8. The drill continues until one of the teams scores ten baskets.

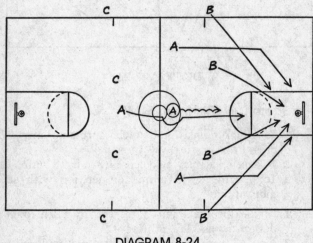

DIAGRAM 8-24

CHAPTER 9 :

Piercing Presses with the 2-2-1 Lineup Attack

WHY THE PRESS?

The outcome of many basketball games is determined by the numerous presses being applied anywhere from full to quarter court.

These man, zone, and match-up presses all focus on today's major skill deficiency—that of ball-handling. Although recent college players have excited the passing world, many players, especially inexperienced ones, still rely mainly on dribbling, rather than passing, for ball advancement. All presses, with their zone-like trapping techniques, thrive on this excessive dribbling.

Presses become even more devastating when applied during a home crowd/court advantage, especially when the pressing team is losing.

Additionally, coaches often try to exploit the value of several quick, defensive-minded team members in order to change the tempo set by bigger teams who may operate strict patterns.

THE LINEUP'S OBJECTIVES

The Lineup Press Attack is based on several sound principles, some obvious and some subtle. Upon careful consideration they all are crucial to the intelligent counterattack of presses. Coaches, sooner or later, will "Meet the Press"—they'd better be ready. The following key thoughts form the backbone of the Penetration's Lineup philosophy.

1. *It reduces trapping opportunities.* The Lineup Attack creates few actual double-teaming chances as all key passes are both short and straight ahead. The dribble is used to encourage trap formation. The easiest pass is then angled away from the rotation of pressure. Good passing triangles are kept consistent with the Lineup's spread "W" set.

2. *It simplifies teaching.* This easy-to-teach attack builds confidence among players as its Side-Center-Seam concept is quickly understood. The alignment and its attack can be well-executed with players having average skills. Furthermore, the same Lineup techniques are used both from the sideline and when facing half-court pressure.

3. *It combines the fast break and press attack philosophies.* Players understandably seek familiarity of basketball concepts. The Lineup blends smoothly with the fast-break principles. The common coaching language used in teaching both the break and press offenses tends to reinforce each area of the game.

4. *It can either actively or passively destroy all presses.* The Lineup can be executed by either aggressively running the ball or patiently walking the ball through the press. Coaches with strong ball-handling talent and board control may choose to push the ball upcourt quickly and score. Conversely, the squad with minimal quickness and overall inferior talent may choose to play the control style of the Lineup Attack. Additionally, within any game, regardless of talent, there is a time to walk and a time to run against the press. The Lineup has this versatility.

The Lineup with its spread "W" set can attack any type of press be it a man, zone, or match-up in structure. There is no need to change the alignment when facing multiple presses.

5. *It forces a five-player offense.* It is important that all defenders closely guard each offensive player as all Lineup attackers are equally potential threats to cripple the press. Each player is assigned a spot in the Side-Center-Seam approach and will automatically play a vital role in destroying the press.

The Lineup's spread set eliminates the concealment of any weak defenders as usually the best defenders are assigned to the primary ball handlers. This frees the remaining Lineup attackers to isolate the weaker defenders.

THE LINEUP'S "W" SET AND PERSONNEL

The phrase "Lineup" serves a dual role. It is both a vocal alert and a visual reminder of the press attack's look. It is signaled either from the bench or from the court whenever a press is seen forming. Two players are lined up in the backcourt just inside the midcourt line. A third player, a guard, will eventually join the other two, making a three-player "lineup" across the midcourt line.

The Lineup presents an unorthodox set in that all five players begin in the backcourt. They are positioned in a "W" as shown in Diagram 9-1 and remain in that spread set until the traps are sprung and the fast break is underway.

This odd information forces individual man-to-man defensive coverage of all five players both before and after the ball is inbounded. It is especially tough to defend as all players are but one pass from each other. Each is also poised in practiced fast-break lanes waiting for that first attempted trap which signals the break from midcourt. At the very least, a 3 on 2 advantage will materialize.

Player 2, the center or tallest forward, is the inbounder. He is the only player assigned to inbound the ball from either the baseline or sideline. Placing the center-forward in this critical spot may appear to be a gamble to some but experience has shown that his movements are restricted to three basic roles. Player 2 must be able to:

1. Swing the ball to the weak side.
2. Fill the normal trailer roles in the fast break.
3. Serve as a defensive intimidator while delaying a reversed fast break.

Being tall, the center-forward also has good court vision that enables him to see over approaching traps. He can then pass above them with the high two-handed snap pass. Player 2 is also drilled constantly on the delaying tactics of the 2 on 1 and 3 on 2 defensive break situations.

Players 1 and 4 are the guards. One of them, player 4, is the middle man best skilled at running the fast break. After the ball is inbounded, 4 rolls to his middle spot as 1 teams up with 2 in the backcourt to begin the attack. Diagram 9-1 shows 4's position after he has rolled to the middle of the court in the center circle. This vital cut will be described later in further detail.

Players 3 and 5 are usually forwards who fill the outside break lanes. It is important that both 3 and 5 have good pass receiving skills

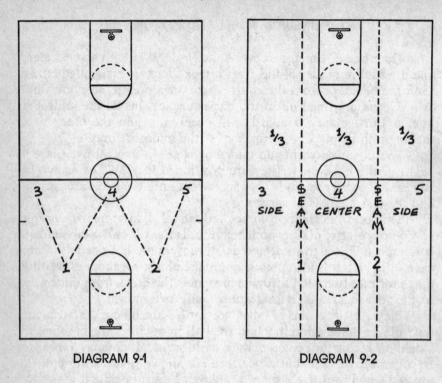

DIAGRAM 9-1   DIAGRAM 9-2

with 3 being either a lefty or having at least adequate control with his left hand.

SIDE-CENTER-SEAM CONCEPT

This theory is a simple teaching device that clearly shows each player his "W" positioning and subsequent movements. Tell your players to split the court lengthwise into three equal lanes. The two outside lanes are called "sides." The middle lane is called the "center" and the two imaginary lines (they are shown as dotted lines in the diagram) that split each third of the court are called "seams." Diagram 9-2 shows this court division along with all court labels. This diagram also shows all five areas being occupied.

Forwards 3 and 5 each fill a side lane with their backs to the sideline providing them with maximum court vision of their teammates and total visual awareness of potential blindside defenders who may try to rotate up for steals or deflections. They are positioned about three feet in from the sideline and the midcourt line.

Guard 4, the middle man in the center lane, also faces the ball but keeps his back to the midcourt line. He, too, stands in the backcourt within the center jump circle.

Backcourt players 1 and 2 must divide the court into thirds and place themselves exactly on a seam. Player 1 is shown on the left seam as 2 stays on the right seam. Both seams are interchangeable as the inbounder must fill the vacant seam opposite the inbounds pass. This simple, but crucial, principle positions both of them within easy passing range of the other four points of the now established "W."

This Side-Center-Seam concept is maintained over a full-court basis so the language is clear and consistent for all players. This full-court consistency also solidifies the familiar image of the letter "W" in the Lineup set and the fast-break picture.

Good coaching is good teaching and well-chosen phrases help both areas. Phrases, if selected carefully, can "light the bulb" for athletes. They can understand and react quickly if key thoughts with minimum syllables are presented. For instance, we use the term "center" as both a court position and an action verb. It was borrowed from soccer coaches who constantly implore their wings to "center" the ball. It is our standard term used in teaching both our Lineup press offense and our fast-break game. "Center it!" is much quicker and active than the familiar, "get the ball to the middle!" Good coaching includes this constant search for clear yet visually active terms and phrases.

THE LINEUP VS. FULL-COURT MAN PRESSURE

The Lineup Attack effectively attacks the man press because its first option is the quick inbounding pass to a streaking forward near half court. This is often available after a team scores while they are busy passing out credits for the score. These opportunities present themselves several times each game and should always be explored.

If the "bomb" is not there, a two-player stack move springs open the best handling guard and clears out a section of the floor for his isolated dribbling.

After the opponents score, inbounder 2 takes the ball from the net and runs to a spot just outside the lane extended, as shown in Diagram 9-3. Player 2 must be trained to always look upcourt from the moment he retrieves the ball so he can instantly read the defense. If a press is being applied he yells "Lineup!" The inbounder's first look

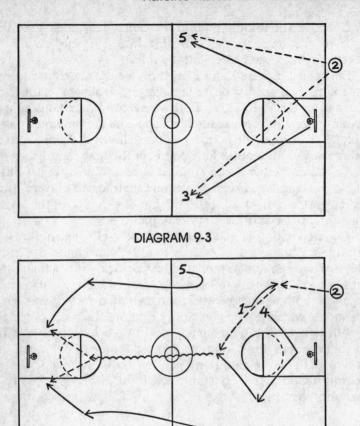

DIAGRAM 9-3

DIAGRAM 9-4

is long to either 3 or 5 who have sprinted to midcourt. If no quick
midcourt pass is available, forwards 3 and 5 remain in their side spots
with their backs to the sideline. It is important that 2 clears the lane
extended when out-of-bounds so the backboard won't limit his
crosscourt pass to forward 3.

Meanwhile, guards 1 and 4 have stacked at the free throw line
extended. They are directly facing inbounder 2, as shown in Diagram
9-4. Back guard 1 places his hand on the side of 4 and pushes him in
one direction toward a sideline as 1 follows by cutting up and then
toward the opposite sideline. Player 2 then passes to either 1 or 4.
Following his pass, 2 goes to the seam opposite the ball and stays
slightly behind the ball's position. The guard who didn't receive the

inbounds pass (4 in Diagram 9-4) then makes a center cut down the center lane looking for the guard's pass. This center cut tests the defensive structure for its man or zone qualities.

If 4 is open, he receives the pass from 1 and looks for forwards 3 and 5 who have jab-stepped up and broken long. Player 4 then runs the standard 3 on 2 fast break with 3 and 5 who are running down their preassigned lanes. Players 1 and 2 remain on both seams to trail this break attempt or stop a reversed fast break.

If guard 4 in Diagram 9-5 is covered during his center cut, he simply stops at his center spot in the circle. He turns to face the ball and actively flashes to meet any centering pass from either of the two seam players.

TRAILING THE GUARD

Diagram 9-6 shows 1 dribbling the ball upcourt while facing singular man pressure. Inbounder 2 has filled his own seam but remains about two steps behind the imaginary line of the ball as 1 advances it upcourt. Our off-ball guard on the seam is trailing properly if he maintains this key position just behind the Ball Line. It is a vital position as it provides guard 1 with an easy release pass from a closing trap.

SPACING THE "W" SET

All five points of the "W" must keep the spacing constant as the ball moves upcourt. This moving "W" keeps its perfect passing

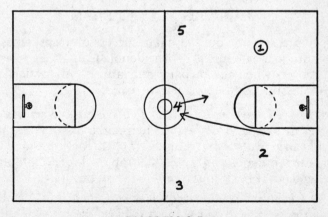

DIAGRAM 9-5

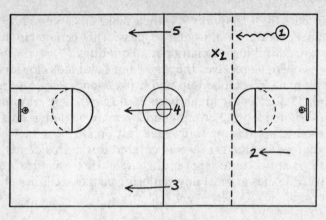

DIAGRAM 9-6

triangles, which gives a steady attack or release valve for the dribbler. The "W," if maintained, also preserves the fast-break formation. Spacing is done as soon as dribbler 1 (Diagram 9-7) is slightly past the top of the key but before the ball reaches the hash mark. The 3-4-5 Lineup, when the ball is just past the top of the key, then moves as a straight line into the frontcourt at the same speed as 1 is advancing. This team movement maintains the same easy passing distances and angles as in the backcourt. It is necessary that 3,4, and 5 move away as the ball is dribbled toward them. This prevents their men from congesting the area or double-teaming the dribbler. Notice that the distance between the ball and the 3-4-5 Lineup *before* the dribble (broken lines) is the same as *after* the dribble during its advancement.

HANDLING THE DOUBLE-TEAM

Most presses are built around successful traps whose main functions are to create mistakes. The double-team or trap has caused many turnovers when players panic and attempt unpracticed skills. A trap is successful for three primary reasons:

1. *A trapped player puts his back to the defense.* When the double-team pressure tactics become too intense, the ball handler picks up his dribble and pivots away from the trap. This action places his back to his open teammates and forces the trap to close even tighter, thus preventing a pivot back to the original position.

2. *The dribbler stops his dribble too early.* When the dribbler sees the oncoming second trapper about to close the trap, he often picks

up his dribble, allowing them to attack more aggressively. They then harass the guard and block his passing vision. A player should never stop the dribble unless he is sure he can shoot or pass immediately.

3. *The ball handler attempts an unpracticed pass.* Because of a possible time factor combined with the natural crowd and score problems, a player may either throw the ball into a crowd or out of the gym.

It is crucial that all players learn these three common reasons for successful traps. Additionally, the coaching staff must drill repeatedly on the handling of traps.

Initially, the ball handler must face the oncoming trap by backing off it briefly while using two or three backup dribbles. This provides extra time to avoid the actual trap and to see an open teammate.

The backup dribble also eliminates the second problem of facing traps, namely, the stopped dribble. The dribble is now continued while backing up and spotting open teammates in the Lineup or the trailing guard.

The best pass to beat traps is the high two-handed snap or "top" pass. This is especially valuable when used by center-forward 2. Practice this pass constantly in your Lineup attack drills. This pass is also used as an outlet pass to start the fast break along with the crosscourt pass in attacking dropback zone defenses. It is very effective in beating the press as the ball fake from this high position can easily move the defenders by first faking toward one of the Lineup players, keeping the ball, and then passing to another.

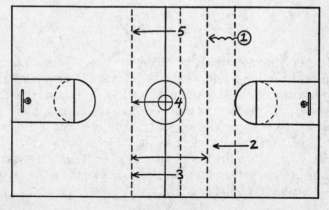

DIAGRAM 9-7

The teaching drills for handling traps are covered at the end of the chapter with the other lead-up drills.

FACE THE PRESS— MAKE THE EASIEST PASS— TARGET HANDS

Diagram 9-8 shows a man press with a normal trap and a helpside rotation. X5 has rotated up to trap guard 1 with X1. Guard 1 takes 2 or 3 back dribbles. This backing movement keeps the Lineup players within passing range, providing him extra time to spot the open receiver. If X4 has rotated to cover 5 and X3 has moved to cover middle man 4, then forward 3, with his back to the sideline, breaks up court with a high target hand for 1's high two-handed snap pass. We use the high target hand as a signal that we want the ball thrown long to us. The cutter's high hand target signals the passer he wants the ball. Quick backdoor cuts with no target hand are only fakes and no pass should be thrown.

When the high top pass is thrown to the Lineup's weakside cutter, it should result in a lay-up, as all defenders are rotating in the backcourt. The dribbler has some basic thoughts to consider. He must face the trap, back dribble, and make the easiest pass to a cutter's target hand breaking into the frontcourt. If any one defender in the Lineup goes up to trap, regardless of the defense used, one of the Lineup players has to be open for a top pass and a lay-up.

SEAM TRAP

The only other area that dribbler 1 (or 2) can face trapping pressure is from the trailing guard's defender. Diagram 9-9 shows X2 sliding laterally to double-up dribbler 1 with X1. Player 2 must first vocally warn his backcourt mate of the coming trap. Just before the trap is set, 1 backs up, if necessary, then releases to unguarded 2. Player 2 then dribbles upcourt as the Lineup pushes the still intact and spaced "W" into the frontcourt. Dribbler 1, before passing, must maintain possession as long as possible to guarantee he can still throw the easiest available pass.

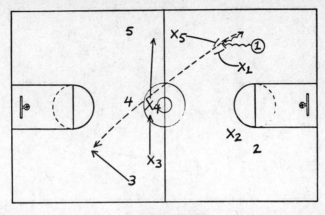

DIAGRAM 9-8

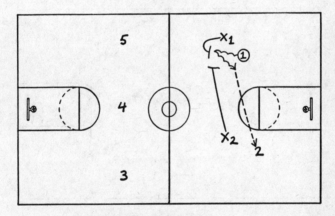

DIAGRAM 9-9

LINEUP VS. THE RUN AND JUMP

Diagram 9-10 shows the Lineup against the popular run and jump defense. Here 1 tries for a delayed look by facing the forming trap and taking 2 or 3 back dribbles. This effectively stalls the trap and still keeps the 3-4-5 Lineup within passing range. Dribbler 1 now makes a high snap pass to either 3, 4 or 5—whichever breaks into the frontcourt with the high target hand signal. Player 2 must also read the defense and vocally alert 1 for the open cutters. Again, no member of the Lineup breaks long with the target hand signal unless his

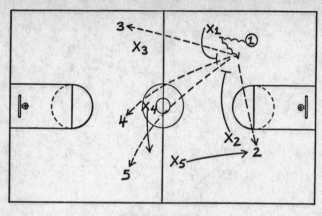

DIAGRAM 9-10

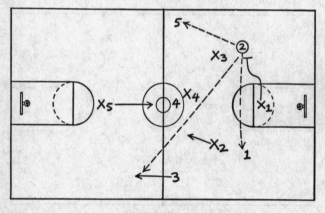

DIAGRAM 9-11

nearest defender has rotated and he is open. Guard 1 can also pass to seam guard 2 if he is open.

LINEUP VS. ALL ZONE PRESSES

Today's zone presses are also geared to stopping the guard, or guards, by double-teaming the ball and by discouraging the two nearest release players from receiving the ball. The Lineup's primary objective is centering the ball and then reversing it to the weak side before the defense can adjust.

All zone presses will show either an odd or even front. The

Lineup defeats either press, providing the easiest pass on the court is the main attacking weapon.

ATTACKING THE ODD FRONT ZONE PRESSES

Diagram 9-11 shows the Lineup attacking the odd front 1-2-1-1 or *diamond* zone press. Presses giving the same slides and action to this diamond press are the 1-3-1 or 1-2-2 formations.

As 2 dribbles the ball along his seam he awaits the inevitable trap coming from X3 and X1. As the trap starts to form, 2 backs up his dribble and releases to the open man. This will be either to his backcourt teammate 1 or one of the other Lineup players. The diagonal weakside area occupied by forward 3 is usually open. The diagram also shows the diamond's standard rotation and the Lineup's release and attacking passes. The ball being entered on the offensive left seam would usually find forward 5 open on the opposite diagonal.

LINING UP THE
EVEN FRONT ZONE PRESSES

The Lineup attacks the even front 2-2-1 or box press with the same spread set. No change in the Lineup is really needed when facing the multiple press formations.

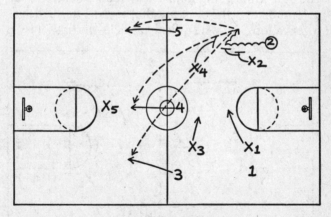

DIAGRAM 9-12
2's Backup Dribble
and Three Possible Passes

As shown in Diagram 9-12, the ball is inbounded following the optional stack and 4's center cut through the middle. Inbounder 1 has filled his seam as 2 dribbles downcourt. X2 is influencing his path to the outside using the sideline as an extra defender. As 2 sees X4 rotating up for the trap near the time line, he backs up his dribble and passes to either middle man 4 or to weakside forward 3, whichever is open. Lineup player 5 may also be open if X5 comes up to help out on either 3 or 4. The standard 2-2-1's slides can't cope with the 3-4-5 Lineup across the midcourt.

THE "GO LONG" OPTION

If some of the second line defenders on either the diamond or box presses are slower than the offensive players, we use the "Go Long" option to capitalize on their deficiency.

Diagram 9-13 shows the Lineup facing a normal 2-2-1 box press with either X3 or X4 lacking agility or quickness. As guard 2 is dribbling the ball upcourt, he yells "go long" to forward 5, who is directly in front of him. Forward 5 then jab-steps toward the ball and breaks long into the frontcourt. This places added pressure on deep defender X5, who must now decide on either stopping the immediate threat 5 or the potential centering pass to middle man 4.

As forward 5 is breaking long, 3 jab-steps upcourt and flashes toward the ball while going toward the sideline. Player 2 can pass to 5 breaking long or to 3 flashing parallel toward the ball.

If 5 gets a long pass, he quickly attacks the basket for a lay-up. If

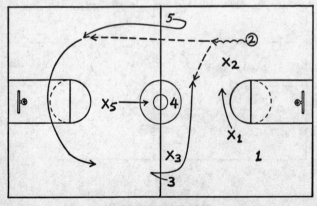

DIAGRAM 9-13

3 gets 2's pass, he takes the middle of the court as 4 fills the empty lane. If 5 doesn't get the ball, he breaks back toward 3's original side and 3 likewise replaces forward 5.

If neither pass develops, 2 can still pass to 4 or reverse the ball to trailing guard 1. Guard 1 can now look for forward 5 coming back high from his first long cut or for 3 flashing back toward the ball.

If the ball was being handled by 1, the roles of 3 and 5 would be reversed. Player 3 would then break long and 5 would flash toward the ball. This change is shown in Diagram 9-14.

Player positioning is a bit different for the Long option. You can play any left-hander in the 5 spot to utilize his strong hand while dribbling, following his flash to the ball. If 2 has the ball and 5 runs long and then crosses over, he is again using his dominant hand for any lay-up attempt. The right-handed player is then assigned to the 3 spot for the same reasons as just mentioned.

If you have an exceptionally poor ball handler or receiver, position him in the middle position 4. Players 1 and 2 are to center the ball to him during the Long options only if there are clearly no defenders in the middle lane near receiver 4. He then holds it high until an open teammate can get open for a release pass.

The Long option is valuable in many situations, especially as a change-of-pace against teams that press constantly.

ATTACKING THE HALF-COURT ZONE TRAPS

When facing a half-court press, it is imperative that each player goes to the same position that he occupied during the full-court

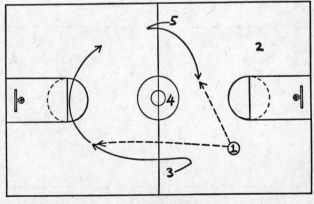

DIAGRAM 9-14

Lineup attack. There is, however, one exception, when the center is already down the floor after his inbounding pass, and the guard has dropped into the backcourt to help the ball handler if necessary. The center is now in the guard's position in the top of the half-circle. The starting positions of the half-court Lineup attack are shown in Diagram 9-15.

Guard 2 again dribbles in his seam toward the baseline. This sends forward 5 to the baseline as he is taught to empty his area when the ball is dribbled toward him. Guard 2 then invites the 1-3-1's trap, which takes the pressure off 5 as a receiver.

Center 1 now drops toward the ballside low post just above the block but stays exactly even with dropping 5. This "teasing" action forces a decision by deep defender X5. He must choose between denying 5 in the corner or defending the approaching post player 1. Guard 2 then has the choice of passing to 5 in the corner or to center 1.

As soon as guard 2 picks up his dribble, weakside forward 3 flashes to a spot *above* guard 2's stopped position. He must wait until the dribble is picked up before he makes his move. This act is familiar to the players as the forward's role is identical to the trailing guard during the full-court Lineup.

Diagram 9-16 shows forward 3 coming high for this pressure release as guard 4 cuts off his back and goes weak side. He can now serve as either a rebounder or as a shooter following a quick ball reversal from forward 3. Any shot attempt by guard 4 is easily rebounded by center low or forward 5 who hustles to the weakside block. The defenders will have a tough time getting any decent board coverage as their trapping efforts will leave them too far from the basket area.

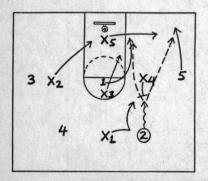

DIAGRAM 9-15

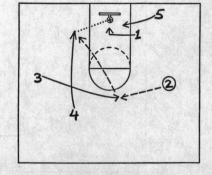

DIAGRAM 9-16

The slides of the half-court Lineup offense are the same if the ball is entered on the offensive left. As the dribbling guard invites the trap, the ballside forward empties to the corner and the center rolls low just above the ballside block. The weakside forward then flashes to a point behind the line of the ball and the off-guard cuts off the forward's tail and places himself in his shooting range. The ball handler can pass to the forward in the corner, the low post, or to the forward flashing high as a pressure release and ball reversal.

One of these options will always produce a good shot and strong board coverage. Also, the ball's quick movement as a result of good angles will discourage future half-court traps.

GUIDELINES FOR
PERFECTING THE LINEUP

Teaching and Practicing Tips:

1. Teach the Lineup during the first practice session. Assume your team will be pressed every minute of every game.
2. Teach the Lineup and fast-break terms together.
3. When practicing the Lineup, get excited when they score.
4. Spend a lot of time on 3 on 2 and 2 on 1 fast breaks.
5. Convey the feeling to the players that they should hope they will be pressed.
6. Guards in their seams must know their primary passing outlets.
7. Know that there are four basic presses the Lineup will contend with and practice against all of them:
   a. Straight man
   b. Trapping man
   c. Zone press allowing inbounds pass
   d. Zone press denying the inbounds pass

Passing Tips:

1. Pass early rather than late.
2. Use high snap fakes; they tend to freeze midcourt defenders.
3. The Lineup is built for *passing* the ball, not *throwing* it. A pass is done right—a throw isn't.
4. It's lay-up time after 2 or 3 crisp passes.
5. Leave your feet to shoot, not to pass.

6. The inbounder should not watch his players, as they are going to the same spots each time. Read the defense.

7. Use ball fakes and change the passing planes often. Always fake the use of one passing plane first and then throw the ball through the opposite plane. This moves defenders either up or down to make the actual pass easier. Fake the bounce to throw the snap pass. Fake the high snap pass to throw the bounce.

Game Situation Lineup Tips:

1. Encourage the guards to smile when seeing the press. It is psychologically damaging to the defense.

2. Keep spacing equal between seam and Lineup players.

3. Don't allow the seam guards to prove their ball-handling ability each time down the floor. Leave some of it unknown.

4. Once the ball is on a fast-break pattern and a defender tries a defensive flick from behind, it is vital that the dribbler perform a quick crossover dribble.

5. Expect a press during the following:
   a. After a time-out
   b. Following a free throw huddle
   c. With the substitution of quick defensive players
   d. When ahead
   e. When pressing

6. Inbounders must back up first to get a look at the sprinting forwards.

7. The Lineup will force a major adjustment to any team's press.

8. If the fast-break attempt fails to produce a good shot, just make a quick back pass and then attack quickly during the defense's natural extension as they are susceptible to the drive.

9. Dribble as far as the defense will allow.

10. Teammates must talk to warn ball-handlers of coming traps.

11. Attack the basket aggressively during the fast break. Don't let the defense reform itself as at least two players will be out of position or in poor body balance.

12. Don't hurry. Wait for the Lineup's perfect passing triangles to show themselves.

13. Many teams press only to see how the coach and his team handle the press. The other coach's assistant will chart your alignment, its moves, and passing routes. Within two minutes a team can judge

how you'll handle future pressure and will either be encouraged or discouraged based on your performance.

14. Take six to eight seconds to cross the time line as most turnovers off presses occur in the first three seconds.

15. If a guard dribbles on his seam toward a Lineup player, that player must empty by moving ahead at the same speed as the guard.

16. Don't take a different shot after attacking the press from what you'd normally be satisfied with from your set offense or fast break.

BUILDING CONFIDENCE IN THE LINEUP ATTACK

Facing and beating today's presses requires as much mental preparation as physical practice. When the two are joined and developed together, the team's performance benefits a great deal.

When teaching the Lineup or any other team maneuver, the introduction comes during a classroom situation using a blackboard or a magnetic playboard. A set of instructions and questions are developed before the presentation in the classroom and are fully carried out during that first session.

Use a set order of increasing competition until the team has learned the movements and can apply them during a preseason scrimmage situation. The steps to learning are as follows:

1. No defense: the team *walks* through the Lineup pattern slowly until it is completely learned.

2. No defense: the team runs the pattern at half-speed.

3. With defense:
   a. Vs. the five slowest defenders at full-speed.
   b. Vs. the best defenders with their hands behind their backs.
   c. Vs. the girls' varsity team as they work their presses against the boys.
   d. Vs. the boys' JV team.
   e. Vs. six, then seven, defenders all pressing together.
   f. Vs. an organized team during a preseason scrimmage.

Space and Face Drill (Diagram 9-17)

WHY: 1. Conditioning and proper spacing.
        2. Defensive slides.
        3. Fast break attack.

4. Dribbling and facing upcourt.

HOW: 1. Players 3-4-5 form the Lineup with 3 and 5 facing in and in their side lanes.
2. Player 4 faces approaching seam guards 1 and 2 who are dribbling upcourt.
3. Players 1 and 2 dribble upcourt using only crossover or behind-the-back dribbles while *always* facing upcourt.
4. As 1 and 2 each dribble upcourt, 3 and 5 must run (glide) sideways as they do during defensive slides. They must face in during their whole trip upcourt like they do during the Lineup attack.
5. Player 4 backpeddles while in the center.
6. When 3, 4, and 5 reach the far baseline they must wait for guards 1 and 2 to reach the baseline. Then 3, 4, and 5 sprint to half court looking back for a possible pass from either guard 1 or 2. After reaching half court, they slow down and resume their defensive slides as they wait for the guards.
7. On the return trip, 1 or 2 will pass (on coach's directions) to 3, 4, or 5 and the three of them will run a standard fast break using three lanes.
8. A new lineup of 3-4-5 will step on the court with new 1 and 2 seam guards.

TIPS: 1. The coach must secretly designate to either of the two waiting guards the one who will pass to the Lineup players for the return trip 3 lane break.
2. Lineup players must constantly be reminded to keep the proper spacing between them and the approaching two seam guards.

Touch and Go Drill (Diagram 9-18)

WHY: 1. To develop inbounder's quick inbounding skills.
2. To develop 3 and 5's abilities to sprint long while looking back.

HOW: 1. Inbounder 2 is directly under the basket with the ball.
2. Forwards 3 and 5 line up even with the dotted line inside the lane with their defenders X3 and X5 beside them outside the lane.
3. As 2 shoots, 3 and 5 sprint to their respective edges of the backboard and jump to touch the corner of the board.
4. Defenders X3 and X5 must sprint to the baseline, touch it, and try to catch up with their assigned players as they break upcourt.

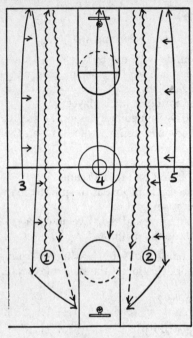

DIAGRAM 9-17

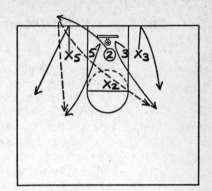

DIAGRAM 9-18

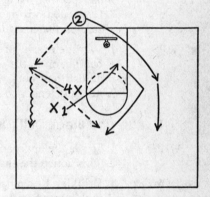

DIAGRAM 9-19

5. Meanwhile, 2 has retrieved the ball from the net and raced out-of-bounds to inbound the ball long to either 3 or 5 as each sprints to his midcourt spot.

6. X2 must rush to tap the backboard and then follow inbounder 2 to pressure his pass by playing his eyes and dominant throwing arm.

7. Player 2 will throw long to either player he can and the forwards will aggressively attack the basket against the two defenders.

8. Continue the drill using six new players.

TIPS: 1. Vary the starting points using the foul lane marking lines. Place either the offense or defense on different lines in order to simulate game-like conditions based on your players' speeds and passing abilities.

Stack Attack Drill (Diagram 9-19)

WHY: 1. To develop timing between inbounder and stack people.

HOW: 1. Player 2 stands out-of-bounds with the ball as 4 and 1 set their stack. Player 1 pushes 4 one way and then he goes in the other direction toward a sideline.

2. Player 2 inbounds to the first open stack player.

3. The cutter without the ball immediately runs the inside center cut, keeping his body between his defender and the passer.

4. Player 4 passes to the cutter if he is open.

5. Player 2 steps opposite the first and to his seam.

6. Players 2 and 4 advance the ball upcourt as the middle man backpeddles using proper spacing.

7. Continue until the midcourt line and then five new players step on the court to continue the drill.

TIPS: 1. Vary defensive pressure on 1 and 4 by playing in front, behind, or on the other side. This forces the stack players to adjust their cuts.

2. Add a defender to inbounder 2.

Lineup and Break Drill (Diagram 9-20)

WHY: 1. To see the approaching trap and to spot the open cutter.

2. To practice the three-lane fast break.

HOW: 1. Dribbler 1 advances upcourt while being guarded by X1, who forces him toward the sideline.

2. Players 2, 3, 4, and 5 are lined up as normal in their spots.

3. Defender X4 is assigned to middle man 4 but the other two defenders are zoning the seams between 3, 4, and 5.

4. As 1 dribbles upcourt, 3, 4, and 5 keep their spacing properly as both Xs stay with them.

5. When X4 chooses he rushes up quickly to trap 1 with X1.

6. Player 1 must back up his dribble, spot the open Lineup player, and pass to him using the high top pass.

7. Whoever receives the pass (3, 4, or 5) must take the center lane of the fast break and the other two must fill the two remaining outside fast-break lanes.

8. When one group completes the fast break attempt at one basket, it turns around and attacks the opposite basket. Following the return trip, new substitutes are added to the drill from the sideline and baseline.

TIPS: 1. On the return trip, have the ball advanced up the opposite side of the floor. This provides sufficient practice of the undeveloped hands both in dribblng and in shooting the fast-break lay-ups.

Top the Trap Drill (Diagram 9-21)

WHY:
1. To teach guards to backdribble while facing an approaching trap.
2. To use the high top pass over the trap.

HOW:
1. Both sides of the court are used by two sets of guards and their respective defenders. The drill is run the same way but in opposite directions.
2. Forwards 3 and 5 are positioned facing in at the midcourt line along with their defenders.
3. It is vital that the two groups of players go in opposite directions to avoid injuries on the scoring end.
4. Player 1 dribbles upcourt against strong man pressure from X1.

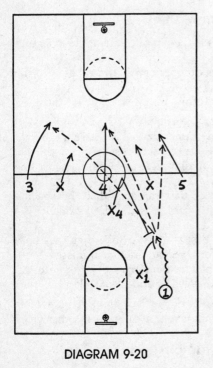

DIAGRAM 9-20

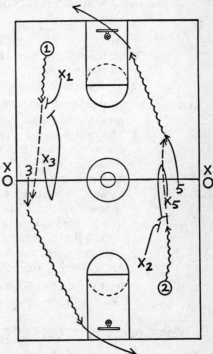

DIAGRAM 9-21

5. As 1 penetrates, forward 3 goes into the frontcourt while maintaining the proper spacing.
6. X3 stays with 3 until 1 gets near the midcourt line. The defender X3 then comes up hard to trap 1 with X1.
7. Guard 1 backs up his dribble and throws a high top pass to 3 breaking long with a target hand for a full-speed lay-up as X3 and X1 chase him.
8. When players complete their turn at one basket, they get in line and go toward the next basket while running the drill in the opposite direction.

TIPS:
1. Give left-handed lay-ups by running the drill on both left sides of the court. They must know how to receive passes and make lay-ups from both sides.
2. Gradually add the middle man 4 and his defender to the drill to further simulate game conditions. His defender is then allowed to rotate toward the breaking forward to force an adjustment to the seam guard.

Space and Roll Drill (Diagram 9-22)

WHY:
1. To develop confidence for the guard in facing the trap and passing out of it.
2. To teach the forward his proper spacing in relation to the advancing guard.
3. To develop the center's timing to roll with the forward.

HOW:
1. The guard dribbles into the trap of a 1-3-1 as the forward maintains spacing by dropping toward the baseline.
2. The center at the high post rolls to a spot just above the block. His defender is not allowed to go beyond the foul line extended.
3. The guard passes out of the trap to either the spacing forward or to the rolling center as the deep defender X4 chooses which to defend.
4. The player having the best shot must take it as they both must follow that shot for a second attempt if missed.
5. Continue drill with a new center, forward, and guard. X2 and X4 switch defensive roles as do X1 and X3.

TIPS:
1. Run the drill on both sides of the floor and alternate while shooting at the other end of your gym on every other day.

Half-Court Swing Shot Drill (Diagram 9-23)

WHY:
1. To develop the weakside forward's flash.
2. To develop the guard's ability to pass from a trap.

3. To improve ball reversal and weakside guard's shot.

4. To stress weakside offensive board coverage.

HOW: 1. Have guard dribble into the trap formed by X1 and X2.

2. The guard passes out of trap to the weakside forward, who has flashed to a point behind the trapped guard.

3. The forward swings the ball to the guard, who has dropped to the weakside directly off the forward's flash.

4. The guard shoots as the forward and the defenders rebound.

TIPS: 1. Run on both sides and ends of the floor.

2. Exchange the guards so each can operate equally well on both sides of the floor.

3. Have X2 release his trap early and hustle to the weak side to pressure the guard's shot.

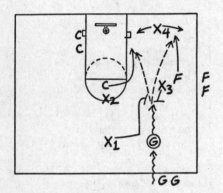

DIAGRAM 9-22

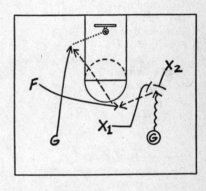

DIAGRAM 9-23

Index